WHAT ARE WE DOING ON EARTH FOR CHRIST'S SAKE?

WHAT ARE WE DOING ON
EARTH
FOR CHRIST'S
Sake?

RICHARD LEONARD, SJ

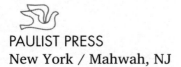

PAULIST PRESS
New York / Mahwah, NJ

Cover image by radoma/Bigstock.com
Cover design by Dawn Massa
Book design by Lynn Else

Library of Congress Cataloging-in-Publication Data

Leonard, Richard, 1963–
    What are we doing on earth for Christ's sake? / Richard Leonard, S.J.
        pages cm
    ISBN 978-0-8091-4902-5 (pbk. : alk. paper) — ISBN 978-1-58768-426-5 (ebook)
    1. Christian life—Catholic authors. 2. Christianity and culture. I. Title.
    BX2350.3.L465 2015
    248.4`82—dc23

                                                      2014040601

ISBN 978-0-8091-4902-5 (paperback)
ISBN 978-1-58768-426-5 (e-book)

Published by Paulist Press
997 Macarthur Boulevard
Mahwah, New Jersey 07430

www.paulistpress.com

Printed and bound in Great britain by
Marston Book Services Ltd, Oxfordshire

To Edward, Chris, Steve, Dan, Christopher,
Lesley & Pat, Jen, Annie & Johnny,
Sally & Justin, Kayleen & Ber, Jill, Ruth & Maurie,
Pamela & Geoffrey, Terese & Paul, Marisa & Philip,
Marlene, Trish & John, Carla & Tony, Marie & Greg,
Pat, Prue & Ben, Beth & Chris, Libby & Paul—
who could ask for better fellow travelers?

CONTENTS

CONTENTS

Contents

PREFACE

Air travel can be both a joy and a risk for a priest. Depending on your point of view and experience, you might judge that I have been blessed or cursed to have to fly so much in my ministry as a Jesuit. Generally, I enjoy it, but I choose to fly under the radar —pardon the pun. I rarely wear clerical dress on a plane, mainly because Australian domestic and international flights are among some of the longest in the world and clerical collars are uncomfortable. Second, the sign of it repels as many people as it attracts; indeed, in secular Australia it can attract unwarranted attention, wherein the attacker has no desire for a conversation, but simply to spew forth bile on me.

Nonetheless, often when traveling in mufti, even before I can get my earphones firmly inserted, a fellow chatty traveler sometimes asks, "What do you do for a living?" St. Ignatius was very keen on the art of the spiritual conversation, and so am I, but not in the sky. Ignatius knew nothing about twenty hours in economy class on planes! In my experience, once my inquirer finds out that I am a Catholic priest, and after accepting that I am who I say I am, the conversation goes in one of five directions.

The first category of responders consists of those who were educated by nuns, brothers, or priests and did not have a happy experience. Those in this group are often lapsed, collapsed, or ex-Catholics. For obvious reasons, if I cut across their tale of woe at this moment, I would only exacerbate the pain and prove their point about the uncaring religious officials they have known. My behavior would become part of their next story. It takes sixteen hours to fly from Sydney to Los Angeles, and four hours into the flight—somewhere over Fiji—I am regularly only up to the third grade with Sister Mary Agapanthus.

The second group comprises those who think I am deluded, that religion is nonsense, and that I believe in Santa Claus, the Easter Bunny, and fairies in the garden. (For the record, I don't believe in any of these three!) These travelers are as vehemently evangelical as any religious fanatic I have met. On one flight, one man, after giving me an earful about my psychological impairments, asked the attendant if he could be moved to another seat. Not only did I not get equal time to respond to my homegrown analyst, my religious belief was so clinicalized that he needed to move before I infected him with the bug!

The third group is among my favorites. It is made up of very conservative Catholics who within three sentences of our conversation know more about the state of my soul than me or my confessor. They have great gifts in regard to knowledge and prophecy, but few in regard to charity, which stems from the fact that I am not wearing a clerical collar. Therefore, they say things like, "Are you ashamed of your priesthood?" No. "Of your faith in our Lord and Savior?" No. "If you wore your clerical dress, you could provide a real witness for this plane, but you are one of those priests who want it all on your terms." Really? I point out to them that we are on a twenty-four-hour flight to London, and I wonder if we would be having this discussion about my clothes if I were a judge, surgeon, soldier, policeman, or pilot. "A priest is a vocation, not simply a job," they reply. My fellow Catholic has not met the extremely dedicated surgeons and policewomen I have the privilege of knowing. Then my interlocutor finds out that I am a Jesuit, and with a roll of the eyes, it is clear that my type of demon can only be cast out by prayer and fasting.

The fourth group is made up of my evangelical Christian brothers and sisters. Don't get me wrong, some of the finest Christians I know are evangelicals, but they can be a bit earnest, and their version of the eye of the needle is the only one through which all camels can pass. On finding out that I am a Catholic priest, they seriously ask me, "Have you given your life to Jesus Christ as your personal Lord and Savior?" "Well, as a matter of fact I have," I reply. "Do you speak in tongues?" "I can, but I choose not to. I don't find it the most helpful form of communication." "Do you know the demands of living the life of the Lord?" Somewhat exasperated now I say, "Listen mate, lifelong poverty, chastity, and obedience for Christ have to be a decent push in the right direction."

Actually, when I say this, I immediately think of the day I took my vows as a Jesuit in the chapel of St. Ignatius College, which is located overlooking Sydney Harbour. After taking my life vows of poverty, chastity, and obedience, my mother came and saw the magnificent sandstone buildings, the skyline of Sydney on the horizon, and the manicured lawns, which led down to the water on three sides of the property. My mother said, "If this is poverty, I want to see chastity. It is looking loose and fast to me." To which I replied, "We are very good on obedience." Actually, I hope we are good at all three!

The fifth group is the most serious: Catholics, Christians, other religionists, agnostics, atheists, humanists, and everything in between, who are as scandalized as I am by the clergy sexual abuse crisis and its cover-up by church officials. Some of these conversations have been worth having, though as the only priest some people have met recently, they could be forgiven for thinking that I had personally committed these crimes and covered all of them up myself. Pent-up rage is often indiscriminate, for we never know when we are going to get another opportunity as good as this one to vent our spleen. I will return soon to the sexual abuse crisis.

A few years ago, the experience of these conversations was so mixed that, when I received my doctorate in cinema studies, I changed my frequent flyer profile from "Father" to "Doctor." On my next long-haul flight from Los Angeles to Sydney, the customer service manager came down to me at row 57. After welcoming me back as "one of our platinum frequent flyers," she said, "If there is anything we can do to make your flight more enjoyable, don't hesitate to ask." So I did. "An upgrade would be nice," I said. She laughed, and walked back to the pointy end of the plane. Her definition of "anything" did not extend that far.

On my next flight to London, down came the customer service manager again, to greet me at row 41 and to make a request. "Dr. Leonard," he said, "There is someone in first class who may need your attention." I explained that, if she was having trouble selecting between the first release or premium movies, then I was her man. In fact, I thought I should get on the PA system and guide everyone through the entertainment offerings. However, if she were sick, I said, I would certainly not be helpful. As he walked away in search of a more immediately useful doctor, I had to stop myself from calling out, "If she goes to God, come back, because I know the prayers for the dead by heart." I restrained myself.

Of all the conversations I have had on planes, however, one of the most memorable led to this book. I was flying from New York City to Los Angeles. As I settled into row 44, a very friendly young man next to me, Thomas, asked me what I did. I told him. He was Catholic. I noted his emphasis was on the past tense, but said nothing. He wasn't sure about anything to do with faith and spirituality. I told him I was a Jesuit, which led him to tell me that he had recently read two books by a Jesuit priest: *Where the Hell Is God?* and *Why Bother Praying?* "Do you know them?" he asked. I looked around for the candid camera. "Yes, I know them very well; I wrote them." He would not believe me until I showed him my business card. This scene was unbelievable.

Thomas and I had a long and engaging conversation about the issues my two books had raised for him, and for me. Although we were as discreet as we could be, some of our fellow passengers must have wanted an emergency landing because of the advanced theology seminar happening at the back of the plane. Tom, thirty, was a highly educated person, an Ivy League graduate. He was also a serious humanitarian, working in Third World countries for Habitat for Humanity during several summer holidays. His wrestle with belief, theology, prayer, and the problem of evil comes out of personal experiences. He told me that as much as he liked my earlier books and found them accessible and helpful, they did not address a fundamental issue for him and most of his friends: the *why* of belief. "We just get worn down by the growing chorus of people who say 'religion is all nuts and you can be a good person and make a difference in the world and not believe anything more than that.' And to say that the Catholic Church has made it very easy to leave in recent years is an understatement." However, Tom wanted more than that. "I can't simply believe that my life, and much more, the people whom I have seen in action with the poorest of the poor, amount to nothing more than the here and now. There must be more purpose to life than that, or at least I hope so." The clincher for me was when he said, "I like reading the Gospels and what Jesus had to say on many things. I think Paul and the others in the New Testament often offer great lessons for life, but I guess what I am struggling with is what are we actually doing on earth, for Christ's sake?"

As soon as Tom said, "For Christ's sake," he apologized, fearing he had offended me by swearing. Not at all! Everything that every baptised person does is meant to be "for Christ's sake." The fact that it has become a throwaway cuss line does not rob the phrase of its original meaning for me. "Why should the devil get the best tunes?" said William Booth, or depending on who you talk to, it was Charles Wesley, his brother John, or George Whitfield.

So this book will wrestle with the profound question that emerged from a chance conversation between frequent fliers somewhere over Arizona: What are we doing on earth for Christ's sake?

Maybe it was providence that I was slow on the uptake with my earphones and met doubting Thomas. As with all sincere searchers, Tom's questions were very good, and like another revelatory event that was shrouded by the clouds, "It was very good to be there."

While I hope this book is intelligent, it is not written for the intelligentsia. Academic treatises do not count for much in most private conversations, classrooms, or even in row 44. So here is an accessible argument for faith. While answering some of the major objections of our detractors, and simply for brevity, while using the more general terms *religion* and *God*, I will primarily be speaking to and about the Christian faith.

ACKNOWLEDGMENTS

I would like to thank the following:

Mark-David Janus, CSP; Paul McMahon; and the team at Paulist Press for their continuing support of my words in the public square;

Brian McCoy, SJ, and the Australian Province of the Society of Jesus for their unfailing belief in my ministry of communicating the Word;

The Australian Catholic Bishops Conference, which supports me in building bridges from our tradition to contemporary culture;

The forebearence of my Jesuit community at North Sydney: Edward, Andy, Daven, Michael, Phil, Aloysious, and Ardi, whose support and care, at home and while away, makes the writing of these books possible.

Chapter One
BELIEF AND UNBELIEF

For Catholics, Stephen Frear's 2013 film, *Philomena*, was necessary but difficult watching. Surprisingly, it ended up being an exploration of some of the causes and effects of contemporary belief and unbelief.[1]

Philomena:	"Do you believe in God, Martin?"
Martin:	"Well, where do you start? That's a very difficult question to answer, isn't it....Erm... do you?"
Philomena:	"Yes..."

[Later, while driving]

Philomena:	"I'd like to stop off and go to confession. We passed a church on the way here."
Martin:	"If you don't mind me asking, why do you feel the need to go to confession?"
Philomena:	"To confess my sins, of course."
Martin:	"What sins? It's the Catholic Church who should confess its sins, not you: 'Forgive me Father for I have sinned. I incarcerated a load of young women against their will and used them as slave labor and sold their babies to the highest bidder.'"
Philomena:	"I just hope God isn't listening to you."
Martin:	"Well I don't believe in God. So, look, no thunderbolt!"

Philomena:	"What are you trying to prove?"
Martin:	"Nothing, just that you don't need religion to lead a happy and balanced life."
Philomena:	"And are you happy and balanced?"
Martin:	"I'm a journalist, Philomena. We ask questions. We don't believe something just because we're told it's the truth. What does the bible say? 'Happy are those who do not see but believe.' Hooray for blind faith and ignorance!"
Philomena:	"And what do you believe in? Poking holes in everyone else? Being a smart alec?..."
Martin:	"I read a very funny headline in a satirical newspaper the other day about the earthquake in Turkey. It said, 'God outdoes terrorists yet again.' Why God feels the need to suddenly wipe out hundreds of thousands of innocent people escapes me. You should ask Him about that while you're in there. Probably just say, 'He moves in mysterious ways.'"
Philomena:	"No, I think He'll just say that 'you're a feckin'eejit.'..."

[At the end of the film when Philomena says she wants to forgive the Sisters who sold her child to adoptive U.S. parents.]

Martin:	"So you're just going to do nothing?"
Philomena:	"No. Sister Hildegarde, I want you to know that I forgive you."
Martin:	"What? Just like that?"
Philomena:	"It's not 'just like that'! That's hard. That's hard for me. I don't want to hate people. I don't want to be like you. Look at you."
Martin:	"I'm angry!"
Philomena:	"It must be exhausting."

Philomena may have taken liberties with the story it tells for dramatic effect, but it is substantially and shockingly true. Through it, there is just no denying that the sexual abuse and maltreatment of children is the greatest contemporary stumbling block to many people having or keeping faith in God and his followers, especially in the Catholic Church. No matter what great good we have done or presently do for a large number of people all over the world, our detractors will quickly say, "Yes, that's all well and good, but what about the sexual abuse crisis?" I want to return to this crisis later, but there is no point starting a contemporary exploration of belief and unbelief anywhere else.

On their side of the belief divide, the problem is that, like *Philomena*'s Martin, people who are aggressive atheists are often not good personal advertisements for nonbelief. Their explicit anger and their snide dismissals must be exhausting. Indeed, as their general category suggests, being an unbeliever is defined by the negative, both in what they say and often in who they appear to be.

With the exception of Alain de Botton, my experience of listening to lectures by the new aggressive atheists like Sam Harris, Richard Dawkins, Daniel Dennett, and the late Christopher Hitchens, leaves me with no hope, even while I agree with some of their criticisms. Their take-no-prisoners approach is so regularly built on cynicism, raw anger, and trading in stereotypes, that I have come to conclude that they can be as fundamentalist and seemingly infallible as the religious edifices they build up to knock down. At gatherings of atheists, religion is not the only tyranny in the room.

It is a pity that the poster boys for aggressive atheism are so unlikeable. And in passing, I want to note that there are presently next to no women leaders emerging out of this movement. Unrelenting negativity is a trial for everyone, and when applied to people who attack religion, it leaves me asking, I know what you are against, but what are you for? If it is removed, then what will take its place? Many aggressive atheists would say "being rational," which supposes that every position, other than their own, is irrational, but more on this soon.

THE COMMON GROUND

Whether some people like it or not, religious belief plays a very important role in nearly every society on earth. It needs to be said at the outset, however, that you do not have to be religious to be a moral person. Some of the finest-living people I know are atheists or agnostics or secular humanists. Clearly, religion does not have the market cornered on ethics. There is enough hypocrisy to go around for everyone. While it was once seen that living the moral life was primarily promoted in terms of earning heaven and avoiding hell, much more nuanced developments in moral theology over the last fifty years or more have moved away from the reward/punishment paradigm to Christians living what they believe to be a response to Christ's invitation to have life, and live it to the full.

Like all humanity, we often sin and fail, but we try to be moral because we are drawn by love, not driven by fear. However, it is striking how most aggressive atheists prefer to keep referencing the reward/punishment paradigm as the only and dominant one in Christianity today. Along with many fellow Christians, I have long left behind the punishing policeman-God, with the long white beard in heaven, the "sky Daddy," ever ready to catch me out and send me to the hell fires. Theology has positively moved on, but that does not fit our opponent's preferred narrative and agenda.

Sometimes, I think some aggressive atheists are railing against their Sunday school teachers from the 1950s. They are entitled to do so, but most Christian theology has matured in the light of contemporary biblical studies, psychology, social sciences, and even in the shameful face of the criminal behavior of the worst of our members. In my direct experience, aggressive atheists resent it when people state, "Well, we certainly used to preach the position you have just outlined, but we don't anymore." Furthermore, in outlining a more recent or nuanced theological position than the one just presented, it is dismissed as, "How very convenient," or "That's just your opinion," or "Well, you held the old belief for a very long time." Apparently, for some of our detractors, no matter what new insights now inform our faith and its articulation, we are not allowed to move from the position that they seek to attack.

Several atheist scholars have provided very helpful challenges to institutional religion. However, some atheists argue as though all religions are monolithic in their condemnation of the modern world, their oppression of human rights, and their negativity to all social developments. This stereotype might have been more true of mainstream Christianity once, but it is far from true now.

Believers and atheists can find common ground in regard to the love of others and the love of self. Most people want many of the same things for the world: kindness, truthfulness, care for the earth, justice, peace, and love, just to name a few. We are sometimes divided over how we can best realize these things, and are always divided over whether our moral choices and ethical behaviors have an impact beyond the here and now. Nevertheless, the fastest growing group in Western society is that which holds no religion at all. Within this group, the rise of those who are antireligion, secular humanists, or aggressive atheists is changing the discussion about what we believe, how we live out that belief, and the context within which we share values.

DIALOGUE WITH ATHEISTS CAN BE CLARIFYING

We need to take our atheists friends very seriously. Believers ignore, resent, or dismiss them at their peril. Again, we are in good company. On October 1, 2013, *La Repubblica*'s founder, Eugenio Scalfari, a public atheist, interviewed Pope Francis:

> "Some of my colleagues who know you told me that you will try to convert me." He smiles again and replies: "Proselytism is solemn nonsense, it makes no

sense. We need to get to know each other, listen to each other and improve our knowledge of the world around us. Sometimes after a meeting I want to arrange another one because new ideas are born and I discover new needs. This is important: to get to know people, listen, expand the circle of ideas. The world is crisscrossed by roads that come closer together and move apart, but the important thing is that they lead towards the Good....Each of us has a vision of good and of evil. We have to encourage people to move towards what they think is Good."[2]

Apart from those who call us insane, poisonous, and dangerous, not all of our detractors wish us ill. They just cannot or will not accept that any claim to religious belief fulfills their definition of rationality. Some atheists do not reject the notion of God outright, but they find the ideas about *a* God—any God—proposed so far in the human community totally unsatisfactory both intellectually and personally. In fact, I readily concede that in regard to every God outside of Judeo-Christianity, I am a respectful atheist myself.

Against what most Christians would think of atheists, I argue that some of their challenges to religious bodies are very good indeed, demanding greater clarity in our thinking; demanding a case for the rationality in religious belief; seeking the case for the right of religious groups to have influence over laws, behavior, and ethics beyond their own faith community; and placing the spotlight on whether we practice what we preach.

No one likes scrutiny. "If you, O LORD, should mark iniquities, who could stand?" (Ps 130:3). Although it is sometimes demanded in the most provocative and accusatory of ways, and may indeed come from those who mean us harm, it does not take away from the fact that being asked to account for ourselves is fit and right. Jesus himself believed in such transparency: "For nothing is covered up that will not be uncovered, and nothing secret that will not become known. What I say to you in the dark, tell in the light; and what you hear whispered, proclaim from the housetops" (Matt 10:26–27). Furthermore, Jesus was the model of openness: "I have spoken openly to the world; I have always taught in synagogues and in the temple, where all the Jews come together. I have said nothing in secret" (John 18:20).

We recall that Jesus' first disciples were sent out to a hostile world and had to pay a price—sometimes the ultimate price—to witness to Christian faith, hope, and love. For some of us, who have become so used to Christianity being afforded respect, it can be disconcerting and dispiriting to encounter people hostile to the way, truth, and life that brings us meaning and hope. We might need to toughen up in dealing with the world, because Jesus never told us to sit at home and wait for the world to come to us on our terms, or to go out to it when it is ready to receive us with open arms. Jesus sent his earliest disciples out to a world that martyred them; he sends the majority of us out to an increasingly tough environment for religious faith, where we have to stand up for our words and ideas, our values and ethics.

While, as Christians, we should not seek an easy ride in accounting for our belief, one thing that is admirable about most atheists is the sheer confidence with which they support their judgments that there cannot be, and is not, a higher power—anything bigger, greater, or more intelligent in the universe—which many people call God. The same seemingly unshakeable self-confidence can also be on our other side of the belief–unbelief divide: God exists! We know it. End of story. Some believers go further and state that, at best, doubters are mistaken and that they will be damned for all eternity. Even in classical theology this position is wrong. While we are called to make right judgments in the light of faith in regard to thoughts and behaviors, God alone is responsible for salvation, and knows the reasons someone has for unbelief.

Personally, I find the apparent infallibility of both positions confrontational, even unsettling. I have a deep and searching *faith* in and about God. I do not have a deep and searching *certainty*. Furthermore, I remain open to my faith in God developing, growing, and deepening as I reflect on the mysteries before me, both human and divine. In good company with St. Anselm, I have a faith that seeks to understand.

No doubt, there are true stories about atheists making deathbed conversions or that "there are no atheists in fox holes," but these days one hears very little of this last-gasp epiphany. In his posthumously published book *Mortality*, the late Christopher Hitchens, who died from cancer at the age of sixty-two, seemed determined to die just in case God was given any credit for his recovery. "What if I pulled through and the pious faction contentedly claimed that their prayers had been answered? That would somehow be irritating."[3]

Of course, there is the story of the atheist who was walking through the woods and said to himself, "What majestic trees! What powerful rivers! What beautiful animals!" As he continued walking alongside the river, he heard a rustling in the bushes. Turning to look, he saw a seven-foot grizzly bear charging toward him. He ran as fast as he could up the path. Looking over his shoulder, he saw that the bear was closing in on him. His heart was pumping frantically as he tried to run even faster. He tripped and fell on the ground. He rolled over to see the bear raise his paw to take a final fatal swipe at him. At that instant our atheist cried out, "Oh my God! Save me!"

Time stopped.

The bear froze.

The forest was silent.

It was then that the famous bright light from heaven shone upon the man, and a voice from the sky said, "Let me get this right. You deny my existence for all of these years, teach others I don't exist, and even credit creation to a cosmic accident. But now, in your hour of need, you expect me to save you as a Christian believer?"

The atheist, filled with integrity, as they often are, looked directly into the light, and said, "It would be hypocritical of me to ask you suddenly to treat me as a believer now, but perhaps you could make the bear a Christian?"

"Very well; good idea!" said God. And with that the light went out, and the sounds of the forest resumed.

And then the bear lowered his paw, bowed his head and spoke, "Lord, bless this food that I am about to receive and make me grateful through Christ our Lord. Amen."

And then he ate the man.

THE FREEDOM TO BELIEVE AND NOT BELIEVE

In our pluralistic democracies, Christians always need to defend religious freedom, including the right not to believe. Atheists and agnostics have a right to disagree with everything we hold to be true, and all conversations should be marked by dignity and respect on both sides of the debate about belief and unbelief. The same applies to the way some Catholics and Christians talk to each other, especially in the blogosphere, where some so-called defenders of orthodoxy know everything about theology except that charity is the mother of all virtues!

Let's be very clear that some nonbelievers could not care less about theology. Affording us the same rights, they are happy for us to believe whatever we want, even though they argue that we are irrational and deluded in what we hold to be true.

Their objections are more about the often privileged status religions can have in society in regard to a few legislative exemptions and taxation. While those days are in the past for most societies, it is unfortunate that some of our detractors ignore the contribution religious groups make to cost-effective, not-for-profit, accessible education, healthcare, and welfare. Every day we work with the sick and dying, the poor, with refugees, migrants, asylum seekers, the disabled, those with HIV/AIDS, convicted criminals, and many others who live on the fringe of our societies. Some of our detractors would soon notice these good contributions if we began not to do them.

They object also to the way religion, especially Christianity, is enshrined in our Western culture and laws. We cannot rewrite history, and while this influence is changing in the Western world, it remains true that in a democracy, the majority's worldview should be reflected in its laws and customs. Interestingly, many Christians would prefer to see *more* Christian ethics enshrined in recent legislative movements. It seems that none of us are content!

In order to have an informed discussion or dialogue between atheists and Christians, a few important ground rules need to be established.

CHRISTIANS ARE NOT ALL THE SAME

While Christians all believe in Christ as the Way, the Truth, and the Life, we have very different theologies and ideas regarding that belief. Many atheists criticize Christians for taking the Bible literally. I do not believe the Bible is the literal Word of God and, since the Second Vatican Council, neither does the Catholic Church. Our Sacred Scriptures are not a book of scientific facts; they reveal religious truth, and they cannot err in what we need for our salvation.

Genesis, for example, does not tell us anything about science. It tells us about theology—that God is the ultimate author of creation. Therefore, Catholics, the largest group of Christians in the world—1.1 billion of us—do not, officially, believe the world was created in seven days six thousand years ago. As Pope Benedict taught, "There are so many scientific proofs in favour of evolution which appears to be a reality we can see and which enriches our knowledge of life. But on the other hand, the doctrine of evolution does not answer every question."[4]

One day I am going to write a book entitled *Numerology in the Bible* (that will be a best seller) within which I will recall that almost all numbers in the Bible are symbolic. One, three, seven, twelve, forty, and fifty have specific meanings:

One is the number for the unity of God.
Three is the action of the Lord, on the third day.
There are, in fact, six active days of creation, two mul-

tiples of three, and on the seventh day God has a rest—the oldest labor law in the world. *Seven* is the perfect number.

Twelve always represents the twelve tribes, or the fulfillment, of Israel. There are twelve patriarchs, twelve judges, twelve apostles, and Jesus is twelve when in Luke's Gospel he undertakes his first public ministry. Fulfillment.

Forty is the time of formation: forty years for the Israelites in the desert and forty days for Noah's flood, Jonah inside the whale, Jesus in the desert, and the time between the resurrection and the ascension in Luke–Acts. Formation.

Fifty is the year of Jubilee, usually celebrated only once in a person's lifetime when, among other things, the Israelites would set the slaves free, the fields were allowed to go fallow for a year, and all debts were forgiven. In Luke–Acts it is fifty days from Easter Day to Pentecost. Jubilee.

As Catholics, we have always believed that apart from using the Scriptures in our daily lives, the Bible is a complex collection of books that needs study and careful interpretation.

Now, it seems that I must have the word *pagan* imprinted on my forehead because every time I go near a shopping mall and am minding my own business, I am accosted by our Christian fundamentalist brothers and sisters. Their public evangelization is admirable. In fact, I know very few Catholics who do it. Almost invariably they approach and ask me about my faith. Invariably we get around to the Bible. That's when I warm up to the discussion. "Can I ask you a couple of questions?" "Sure!" "Do you believe that the Bible is literally true in every detail?" "Amen to that," is the stock reply. "Well then, maybe you can help."

"Was the world made in seven days or two? Did the angel come to Mary or Joseph? Did Jesus go to Jerusalem once or several times? Was the sermon on the mount or on the plain? Are there five Beatitudes or ten? Are there ten injunctions in the Lord's Prayer, or are there five? What were the last words of Jesus—in four Gospels we have three versions? On Easter Day did Jesus appear to Peter first or Mary Magdalene? And when did the ascension and Pentecost happen—on Easter Sunday or forty days later?" By this stage a supervisor has normally sidled up to us and suggests that I have "the demon of confusion" in me. I am not the one confused, and some Christians who take the Bible literally can give us all a bad name, and give our attackers a free kick.

It is no wonder why our atheists and agnostic friends think all Christians take the Bible literally, but Catholics don't; nor do many of the other, older mainstream Christian denominations.

ATHEISTS ARE NOT ALL THE SAME

In his book *Atheists: The Origin of the Species*, Nick Spencer argues that a common error is to lump all atheists together, as though they hold the same position for the same reason. In other words, Christians often do to our arguing partners the very thing we complain they do to us. Spencer argues for "atheisms rather than atheism," charting the very different positions that Saint-Simon, Comte, Nietzsche, Russell, Robertson, and Lawrence have expounded. He says that there are at least six major movements within contemporary atheism: High Church, Low Church, Tin Chapel, Auld Licht, Secularist atheism, and that born from d'Holbach.[5] It is beyond the scope of this book to look at each of these traditions in detail, but given that the last category is the angriest of all and because it seems to be the one from which many of the prominent and contemporary aggressive atheists have sprung, it is helpful to look at it in a little more detail.

Born in 1723, Paul-Henri Thiry Dietrich d'Holbach was German by birth and French by adoption. Raised and educated by his stockbroking tycoon uncle, he would later inherit his vast fortune, estates, and title. Baron d'Holbach moved his young family to the United States in 1753. D'Holbach's wife died the following year. In 1754, he sought and gained a papal dispensation to marry his sister-in-law. It would seem that his belief that God had taken (killed) his first wife at such an early age, coupled with the explosion of scientific knowledge during the Enlightenment, as well as the church's often morally bankrupt behavior on every level of French society at the time, led d'Holbach to publish a blistering attack on Christianity in 1791. *Christianity Unveiled* railed against religion for inventing a deity to explain the world, for claiming that the Bible was in any way an explanation of the creation and ordering of the natural world, and for the immorality of the church's leadership and lavish lifestyle. He concluded that the moral development of humanity was hindered by all belief in God, all religious observances, and Christianity, in particular.

In his *Social System* of 1773 and *Natural Politics* of 1774, he outlined an ethical life devoid of religious underpinnings, which, he argued, would liberate humanity from the serfdom of religious belief. He maintained that making the best moral choice comes not from the Bible or dogma, but from making choices that lead to the greatest happiness for oneself and for others. A fierce intellectual character, d'Holbach was equally famous for the goodness of his life, his care of the poor, and his generosity, including, I am humbled to note, offering exiled Jesuits, whom he intellectually despised, refuge in his home in 1762.

However, d'Holbach was a complex character, who vehemently opposed monarchy, hierarchy, and privilege, which is curious given that he always used his own noble title that, along with his vast wealth, he had inherited from his uncle. Not that he was any advocate for democracy. He opposed it too, arguing that the best form of government was of "enlightened men," who had no allegiances to any political systems of the past and had no religion at all. D'Holbach's thinking influenced Diderot, Rousseau, David Hume, Karl Marx, and Thomas Hobbes. They all quote him at length.

In this inadequate thumbnail sketch, we can see why d'Holbach is seen as the philosophical godfather of Christopher Hitchens, Sam Harris, Anthony Grayling, Michael Onfray, Daniel Dennett, and Richard Dawkins. It would be hard to tell which one of these authors, for example, penned any of these lines: "It is thus superstition that infatuates man from his infancy, fills him with vanity, and enslaves him with fanaticism"; "If the ignorance of nature gave birth to such a variety of gods, the knowledge of this nature is calculated to destroy them"; "All children are born Atheists; they have no idea of God"; "Religion has ever filled the mind of man with darkness, and kept him in ignorance of his real duties and true interests. It is only by dispelling the clouds and phantoms of Religion, that we shall discover Truth, Reason, and Morality. Religion diverts us from the causes of evils, and from the remedies which nature prescribes; far from curing, it only aggravates, multiplies, and perpetuates them." D'Holbach wrote them all, and today, they find a very contemporary echo.

What is striking about the background to d'Holbach's angry atheism is that it was born out of a profound grief for his wife's early death and an inability for anyone to adequately respond to his questions about God's role in it. Understandably, looking for answers, he becomes a true son of the Enlightenment, arguing that science alone will provide meaning and advancement. Furthermore, both his profound grief and the explosion of scientific methods and discoveries occurred while many of the Catholic leaders of his day were wealthy despots, who were more interested in maintaining their power and privilege than following the example of Jesus Christ.

On all three levels, some things never change, for just as experience leads to profound religious conviction, the same can often be said for aggressive atheism, which always has a context. Personal experience, a belief that science will answer the important questions of life, and the ability to point out corrupt religious behavior are, more often than not, the starting points for today's preachers of unbelief.

Contemporary atheists owe more to d'Holbach than other systems of atheism, because of the stridency of his criticism and the calls for religion to be completely dismantled. Here we come to an important and extraordinary irony. After the late 1960s and

1970s, where *tolerance* and *peace* became buzzwords, the 1980s saw an international explosion in national, corporate, and personal wealth, at least for some countries, corporations, and individuals. It was also the decade where economic disparity not only grew dramatically, but through modern media, grew very publicly. Phrases like *the third world* and *the haves and have-nots* entered popular discourse to describe nations with dire poverty, high infant mortality, lack of human rights, poor health care and education, high birthrates, and economic dependence on other wealthier countries. The 1980s and 1990s saw the rise of what was called, by internal and external critics, the "decadent West."

On September 11, 2001, the world's consciousness was awoken by terrorists hijacking planes aimed for what they saw as symbols of Western power and wealth: the World Trade Center, the Pentagon, and arguably, albeit unsuccessfully, the U.S. Capitol Building. Nearly three thousand people died. Security for the "haves" has never been the same since. The terrorists were Muslims, who, by following the West-hating fanaticism of Osama bin Laden and the so-called holy wars he declared on the West in 1996 and 1998, owed a greater debt to his distorted political ideology to "destroy and bankrupt" the United States of America, as he put it in his own manifesto, than to him being motivated by the teachings of the Qur'an.

On September 14, 2001, fifty of the most important Islamic leaders in the world for the first time in history made a joint statement, in which they condemned the September 11 attacks,

> We condemn, in the strongest terms, the incidents, which are against all human and Islamic norms. This is grounded in the Noble Laws of Islam which forbid all forms of attacks on innocents. God Almighty says in the Holy Qur'an: "No bearer of burdens can bear the burden of another" (Qur'an, Surat Al-Isra 17:15).... "Whoever kills a human being...then it is as though he has killed all mankind; and whoever saves a human

life, it is as though he had saved all mankind" (Qur'an, Surat Al-Mā'idah 5:32).

One of the many tragic outcomes born on September 11 was the dramatic rebirth of d'Holbach's aggressive atheism, where mutual respect, tolerance, and understanding are jettisoned. In 2004, Sam Harris's *The End of Faith: Religion, Terror, and the Future of Reason* became the first international bestseller of this school. Richard Dawkins came to international prominence in 2006 with his television series, *The Root of All Evil?*, later retitled *The God Delusion*, which became the title of his book that same year. Then, in 2007, even the title of a book by Christopher Hitchens's played with one of the greatest of Islamic motifs: *God Is Not Great: How Religion Poisons Everything.*

One does not need to focus only on the events of September 11 in order to explain the rise of aggressive atheists. The Catholic Church directly contributed to their emergence as well. Though clerical sexual abuse cases emerged publicly in the 1970s and 1980s, they were considered isolated events by immoral and criminal individuals. However, in 1984, the case of Father Gilbert Gauthe in Lafayette, Louisiana, gained widespread coverage in the United States and beyond, and led to many other victims of clergy sexual abuse coming forward to civil and ecclesiastical authorities. By the end of 1990, cases were being reported everywhere in the Western world, especially the English-speaking world. Understandably, these crimes, the criminals, and the cover-ups led to a significant loss of confidence and respect among believers and nonbelievers alike.

In May 1992, the *Boston Globe* first published a story about the sexual abuser Fr. James Porter. The response to that story started an investigation by the newspaper that reached a crescendo in its January 6, 2002, edition. It published the first of a series of articles detailing how the Archdiocese of Boston had protected abusing priests over decades. The diocese denied any wrongdoing during the entire investigation. Once the Boston domino fell, it set off a chain reaction across the United States that left believers and nonbelievers alike incredulous at the number of victims and perpetrators, and the breadth of the cover-up. Boston's Cardinal Bernard Law was forced to resign on December 13, 2002.

In the aftermath of September 11, while an often ill-informed stereotyping of Islam occurred and regularly occasioned the denigration of all religions, at the same time, the news of Catholic clerical sexual abuse broke. In such a context, it was easy for our detractors to portray all religions as mad and bad. It was as predictable as it was unfair.

It can now be proven that from 1970 to 1990, as the West became wealthier, it also became more secular. At the same time, Christianity, the dominant religion in the West, was increasingly sidelined in political and social debates, had difficulty influencing legislation, and saw the numbers of worshipers drop dramatically. It is ironic that, if that had continued, religion's sphere of influence and its claim on the community's imagination would have seen it a much-reduced social institution. As Edmund Burke said on January 29, 1795, "Nothing is so fatal to religion as indifference."[6] In the aftermath of September 11, when many sides wanted to read the events in religious terms, for better or worse religion came back to the prominence of the public square. Coupled with those evil events, the sexual abuse crisis in the Catholic and other Christian churches enabled atheists to claim that all religions, and all their officials, were a social evil that needed to be eradicated. Later, Professor Dawkins would go as far as to say, "What a child should never be taught is that you are a Catholic or Muslim child, therefore that is what you believe. That's child abuse."[7]

The atheist Douglas Murray has summed up the situation neatly:

> The return of religion as a pivotal factor in politics and war is one of the defining features of the age. It is time Paine, Marx and other secular prophets were gently shelved in the stacks...the books that have most

formed the past, and which are sure also to shape the future, are the central texts of the world religions.... You can be in agreement with Professor Dawkins that Adam did not exist, yet know and feel that the story of Eden speaks profoundly about ourselves.[8]

Whether we like it or not, God is back in public debate, fueled in good measure by those who are God's biggest deniers and detractors.

SCIENCE AND RELIGION

D'Holbach and his disciples demonstrate how science has been and remains a pivotal issue in the belief and unbelief divide. Some aggressive atheists claim that believers cannot have faith in both God and science, that we have to choose. However, no matter what they say, we do *not* have to choose between science and faith. Science asks *how* we came to be here. Faith asks *why* we are here in the first place. Science questions the *mechanics*. Faith addresses the *meaning*. They are very different questions. While respectful of those who do not need to address issues of meaning outside their own existence within the natural order, I am certainly not on my own in not being one of them.

First, while it is true that there may be a majority of contemporary scientists who have no faith in God, it is not true to say that science and Christian faith always cancel each other out. Copernicus, Napier, Francis Bacon, Galileo, Descartes, Pascal, Leibniz, Newton, Sedgwick, Main, Mendel, Pasteur, Stokes, Marconi, J. J. Thomson, Bragg, Heisenberg, Mott, Eccles, Barton, and Robert Boyd are just a few Christians who are among the most famous scientists whom the world has known, even though some of them were criminally persecuted for their science by religious groups, the Catholic Church in particular. It is also inaccurate simply to say that in their day atheism was not a viable option. That may be arguable of the medieval and Renaissance scientists, but Halley and Maupertuis were well known for their arguments against any deity in the seventeenth century, and from the Enlightenment onward, atheism among scientists gained wide currency. Therefore, most of the men mentioned above had choices in regard to religious belief.

Furthermore, there are also world famous contemporary scientists who have religious faith. For example, Nobel Prize physicist Antony Hewish stated, "The ghostly presence of virtual particles defies rational common sense and is non-intuitive for those unacquainted with physics. Religious belief in God, and Christian belief . . . may seem strange to common-sense thinking. But when the most elementary physical things behave in this way, we should be prepared to accept that the deepest aspects of our existence go beyond our common-sense understanding."[9]

Sir John Polkinghorne, a professor of mathematical physics at Cambridge, and also a priest of the Church of England, has said, "The more I examine the universe and the details of its architecture, the more evidence I find that the universe in some sense must have known we were coming....There is just one universe which is the way it is in its anthropic fruitfulness because it is the expression of the purposive design of a Creator, who has endowed it with the finely tuned potentiality for life."[10]

Here is how Francis Collins, a physical chemist, a medical geneticist, and the former head of the Human Genome Project summarizes his understanding of the universe: "God's plan included the mechanism of evolution to create the marvelous diversity of living things on our planet. Most especially, that creative plan included human beings."[11]

There is the Templeton Prize winner, biochemist, and Church of England priest, Arthur Peacocke, who argued that the divine principle is behind all aspects of existence and is quoted as saying, "The search for intelligibility that characterises science and the search for meaning that characterises religion are two necessary intertwined strands of the human enterprise and are not opposed."[12]

Finally, Nobel laureate in medicine and physiology Sir Ernst Chain is quoted as saying,

As far as my own actions are concerned, I am trying to be guided by the laws, ethics and traditions of Judaism as formulated in the Old Testament, which are, of course, also the basis of Christianity. I am convinced, and have been for many years, that it is impossible to construct a sort of absolute and generally applicable code of ethical behaviour on the basis of scientific knowledge alone, if only for the reason that our knowledge about the basic problems of life is far too fragmentary and limited, and will always remain so.[13]

ARGUMENTS FROM SCIENCE FOR BELIEF IN GOD

Many Christian scientists hold that there is such balance in creation leading to the evolution of human life and self-consciousness that there must be an intricate intelligence presiding over its order and development, which we call God.

Some scientists go further and argue that the cause of the world is, by definition, scientifically supernatural, because it came out of nothing. That is what the Big Bang theory is about—it just happened. Theists hold that the Big Bang did not come out of nothing but from the primary cause—God. Atheists usually retort that if God is the cause of the causation, which produced the origin of the universe, then, who created God? We hold that if one is going to be the Creator, God, then by definition that Creator cannot be created. God is. A growing number of atheists argue against the Big Bang theory by claiming that there are probably many other universes besides ours. However, at this stage, that is an unobservable and untestable theory.

Other scientists argue for God on the basis of the extraordinary amount of biological information encoded into every organism on the earth, and not just in its detail and complexity, but that so many elements had to combine in synchronicity for the created order we now know to emerge. The scientific evidence would establish that every living thing has an internal cause and an external effect from DNA, RNA, and enzymes throughout the entire universe. Many atheists do not take issue with this. They argue against calling that cause *God*, and the effect *God's creation*. Richard Dawkins states, "The universe we observe has precisely the properties we should expect if there is, at bottom, no design, no purpose, no evil and no good, nothing but blind, pitiless indifference."[14] If he is correct, this is a hell of a universe to believe in! Yet, as William James said, we do not just "tolerate the material," or as Colm Toibin put it, "I find the idea of extinction, personally, to be deeply strange and unimaginable and not something one faces with equanimity."[15]

Many atheists hold that creation is the outcome of random chance. This needs careful unpacking, because believing in randomness is akin to an act of faith. In fact, the leap of faith into randomness is a greater act of faith than our belief in a higher intelligence, God, as the primary ground of creation, for if one single and central element on earth or in the universe were not in place as it is, we would not exist as we do; we would not be here as we are. It is difficult to believe that the complexity and balance in creation, from the solar systems to the unbelievable structure of a cell, are a result of random chance. In 2007, Pope Benedict said, "The question is not to either make a decision for a creationism that fundamentally excludes science, or for an evolutionary theory that covers over its own gaps and does not want to see the questions that must be assigned to philosophy and lead beyond the realms of science. We need both."[16]

Finally, while many of us enjoy looking to science to answer satisfactorily how we are here and from where we came, science cannot answer *why* we are here, *why* life matters, *whether* our life is worth anything at all, and *where* we are headed. Some atheists say that the "why question" is a stupid one to ask, but humans have been asking it for thousands of years. I want it answered, and science is unable to. I do not want to be told that life is meaningless. Faith tells the opposite story. Indeed, our belief tells us where we came from, why we are here, where we are going, and why and how we should live the best and most generous life here and now.

RELIGIOUS EXPERIENCE

A recurring element in the belief and unbelief debate is the centrality of religious experience. Some atheists claim that our religious experience leads one to believe in "imaginary friends," and helps us bolster a fragile sense of who we are and why we are here; that faith is a coping mechanism for those of us who need a crutch to get through life.

We know there is a vocal group of atheists who dismiss all religious experiences and any belief in God as manifestations or symptoms of a psychiatric disorder: "belief pathology."[17] Many of them claim that it is irrational to believe in anything other than that which a scientific method can experiment upon, test, evaluate, prove or disprove, and provide empirical proof for or against.

There are three responses to these challenges. The first is that while it is contested in some circles, many people accept that there are different types of knowledge: the traditional intelligence quotient or IQ, emotional intelligence, social intelligence, and the even more recent and more contested spiritual intelligence, which attends to compassion and creativity, self-awareness and self-esteem, and flexibility and gratitude. So there is more than one way of knowing everything, but more on this topic later.

The second response is that there are many human experiences that we are unable to "scientifically" test but in which we believe and trust. The best example of course is love, especially sacrificial love, where a believer or nonbeliever will give everything, even his or her life, for something or someone else. Some atheists intensely dislike this example, because they claim that computerized tomography (CT scans) and neurotransmitters can chart the effects of love, at least in its chemical and electrical interactive effects in the brain. Of course, the same argument can be made of every emotion. It is just that the experience of love can be totally irrational: what we love, who we love, how we love, and why we love. Love and its effects can be observed, but testing, evaluating, proving, or disproving love as an experience tests the limits of empirical knowledge.

The same case applies to forgiveness, beauty, and conscience. We know these primal human experiences to be real, powerful, and determinative. We rationally know about these realities in our life because we have *experienced* them. On the same basis, some of us know the reality of God because we have encountered God's love. Indeed, for Christians, religious experience is pivotal to our faith. Rather than speak about this in the abstract, let me share my own experience.

Coming from a very devout Irish Catholic Australian family, we are tribal. Growing up, my life revolved around my large extended and smaller immediate family and the local Catholic Church. I went to Catholic grade, intermediate, and high school. My uncle was a priest and many relatives were nuns. Despite my education extending through the rebellious 1970s, I never questioned God or the prerogatives of the Church. I was a proud Catholic, but my relationship was primarily to the tribe—to the Church—not to God. At fifteen, that was soon to change.

The day was toward the end of 1978, when five young Catholics walked into my high school religious education class: Peter, Judy, Maree, Vince, and Peter. They were all older than me, eighteen to twenty-two, and I knew some of them. As soon as they started speaking, I was captivated. They began by saying they had sat where we were sitting. They identified with us as being ordinary young Catholics searching for meaning and purpose. And then they told us how they went on a retreat that changed their lives. It had been put together by a man who was to become a mentor and friend, Fr. Ray O'Leary. The entire retreat was based on the pivotal question in Mark's Gospel: "Who do you say that I am?"

The five young evangelists in my classroom consequently reported having a deep encounter with God and an experience of their faith in Christ.

I had never heard any Catholic, let alone a young adult, talk like this. Not only was their faith unashamedly public, they were palpably, infectiously happy. I knew these people. I could not dismiss them as Jesus freaks or screwballs. They lived up the street from me, and indeed two of the four men had sat in the room where we were sitting only five years earlier. They were happy.

I remember thinking that I had never seen any demonstrably happy Catholics talk about their faith like this. I was hooked.

While making this retreat, we were challenged about our faith, about Christ. We were reassured that God is loving, forgiving, and merciful. It was like I was hearing this for the first time, and it gave me hope and confidence.

There were extended periods of silence, and wonderful prayer sessions, which culminated in a long and life-changing celebration of the Eucharist, after which we were asked if we chose Christ or not. We had a very discreet and Catholic version of an altar call, where, if we chose to step out in faith, we were prayed over. There was no pressure either way. We were explicitly told that we were free to say yes or no, but in saying yes, along with scores of others, I had a religious experience, a flooding of the heart. In fact, I would not be writing this book if it were not for that retreat.

Somewhere in having a religious experience, I went from being in the tribe, to understanding why the tribe exists. I had an encounter with the presence of God.

Atheists often counter with two objections to personal religious experience. First, it's personal and so unverifiable. To an extent, this is true because, generally, religious experiences have the status of private revelations, offering nothing significant for the wider group. Catholicism, for example, is very slow to endorse the experiences per se of mystics. However, it is incorrect to say that the experience is entirely beyond verification, because in almost every case, the experience causes a change in the person's life, often for the better. This is entirely observable. Sometimes these changes are dramatic, sometimes less so, but the change is verifiable. Exactly the same argument can be made about love. Sadly, there are some people who have not or cannot experience love, or who have encountered such evil that love for them is an idea or concept that they hear about from the experience of another person. However, that does not mean that love does not exist, just that they have not had or do not want to have this encounter.

The second objection made in regard to religious experiences is that they lack cross-cultural and multifaith dimensions, and that, because people have different experiences of God, it cannot be one and the same God. Therefore all personal appeals to God are false. This is a category problem. William James, an agnostic, observed that there are four elements to all mystical traditions: ineffability (the experience was often indescribable); noetic metaphysics (the experience revealed something important to the person); transience (the experience did not last and could not be summoned at call); passivity (a sense of being taken over).[18] So while there may be individual differences, there is common ground.

Furthermore and much more importantly, the Islamicist Daniel Madigan is correct in observing that while there are cross-cultural manifestations of mysticism, study of these elements alone ignores that mysticism is "mediated for us by a community and situated firmly within that community's tradition of belief." Madigan does not dismiss the reality of mystical experience or its social and religious importance, but argues it is "firstly an experience of oneself…assenting to or achieving insight into and finally giving oneself over to the vision of reality proffered by a community that lives by that vision." Madigan argues that mystical experience is "not so much a direct experience of God as an experience of believing." He concludes, "If religious experience appears to be a phenomenon common to all traditions, we cannot claim that it is because a single absolute or ultimate is clearly at work in them all. What gives these diverse experiences a tantalizing commonality amid all their differences is the fact that they are all instances of human persons being drawn into communal vision or hypothesis about reality."[19]

It is entirely acceptable to appeal to a personal religious experience when it is understood as being mediated by one's belief, time, space, language, and culture.

If religious experience is irrational, then so are many other fundamental human encounters that give life purpose, meaning, dignity, and beauty. Consequently, appeals to all experiences would be irrational, and not to be trusted. We do not accept this in regard to other encounters like justice, truth, beauty, and goodness. Religious experience falls into the same category and is built on a similar way of proceeding.

DIFFERENT WAYS OF KNOWING

Even within the school of the philosophy of knowledge—epistemology—there are three general and major categories: personal knowledge, procedural knowledge, and propositional knowledge. Religious experience belongs, primarily, to believing in the rationality of personal knowledge through personal apprehension.

It is helpful to note here that there is not just one way of knowing in science either. In *The Emperor's New Mind*, distinguished British mathematical physicist Sir Roger Penrose outlines how scientific theories can be categorized as

- *superb*: where a theory has validity because of its manifold applications and consistency, like general relativity;
- *useful*: where a theory works well enough but fails to be robust in its applications and consistencies, like the Big Bang theory; and
- *tentative*: where a theory lacks "any significant experimental support," as in the case of string theory.[20]

Some atheists claim excessively for scientific knowledge in a way that does not give due regard to the contested and provisional nature of the process. Scientific knowledge can be presented as monolithic, as the only form of rational thought, and dismiss religious knowledge as "at best, a misguided opinion." At the same time, it must be admitted that some believers will wrongly dismiss scientific arguments as "only a theory." Scientific methods, however, emerge through formulation, circulation, resistance, negotiation, conversation, replacement, acceptance, or dismissal. It could be argued that in terms of Penrose's tripartite approach (and religious knowledge may be thought of as "useful" in every way), it is a categorical mistake to want ideas about God and religion to fit scientific theories. Religion lacks the *type* of evidence used by science. This does not necessarily make it irrational or unreal. Religious knowledge appeals to cross-generational individual and collective religious experiences, a life that flows from it, and philosophical reflection upon these things, in a similar manner to the way in which many nonreligious cultural, ethical, and social institutions have developed and emerged as well.

There are limitations to scientific knowledge and its sphere of influence. It cannot answer questions of meaning, create morality, justify itself, or save the world. It is important to note that even with the valuable contribution of science to the causes, effects, and remedies of poverty, hunger, injustice, violence, greed and oppression, scientific knowledge alone has not been able to eradicate these problems. Terry Kelly, a scientist and theologian, neatly summarizes the issues involved.

> When science is considered the lone road to truth, the following dilemmas are confronted:
> - Firstly, science leads to walls which cannot be scaled by science alone. The beginning of the universes and its contingency (it did not have to exist), the progress of the cosmos from chaos to ever more sophisticated organization and its overall fine-tuning cannot be answered without venturing into metaphysical territory.
> - Secondly, whole science delivers us many things for humanity's benefit; it cannot provide the plan and motivation for the human race to actually use things for the benefit of all. It cannot speak of purpose or conscience or of the possibility of anything outside the realm of the material.[21]

Kelly also states that religion cannot be the sole benchmark for all truth. He approvingly quotes Ian Barbour's approach in *When Science Meets Religion* as a way forward for science and religion: "Dialogue may arise from considering the presuppositions of the scientific enterprise or from exploring similarities between the methods of science and those of religion, or from analysing concepts in one field that are analogous to those in the other."[22]

BELIEVERS ARE NOT ALONE

Appeals to numbers can be a fallacy: one million people cannot be wrong! Well, they can be! Certainly, if the atheists of the world were a majority, their objections to numbers would surely not be so strong. However, I focus on numbers for a very specific reason. Religious experience is one of the most multicultural and cross-generational experiences in the human community, but this point should give some pause for thought.

Of the 7.02 billion people in the world, 31.6 percent are Christian, 23 percent Muslim, 15 percent Hindu, 7 percent Buddhist Sikh, and 18 percent comprise all other religions, including our Jewish friends. On the world stage, the nonreligious and the atheists constitute 5.4 percent of the whole world's population. There is no point denying that this last group is now quickly growing in many parts of the world, especially in the West, but the vast majority of the world's people believe in something religious.

An atheist once told me that believing in God is exactly the same as when the majority of the world believed that the earth was flat. Science came and changed it forever. He argued that this is what will happen with the world's population from here on—we will have better education and dump God. His analogy was not the best one for his case. It was experience that changed perception and shaped science. Eventually, everyday people went to the horizon and did not fall off, so the theory was embraced because many people could test it. I do not believe that if you get more money and education, then it necessarily leads to a loss of religious faith. A very high number of religious believers can be found among some very wealthy and well-educated populations in the world.

Aggressive atheists need to be careful that their arguments are not built on the irrationality of self-importance and moral superiority and its inherent intolerance. Christianity has been there, done that, regrets it, and lives with the consequences of it. The present attitude of some atheists could be colloquially expressed as, "If only the poor, dumb religious people of the world were smarter and brighter, then they would throw off the yoke of religion." This is a form of social colonialism, which, if applied to other issues and contexts, would rightly be judged to be objectionable. Sadly, I am more than aware that some uncharitable believers offer a reverse variation on a similar theme to our nonbelieving friends—both positions are to be avoided.

Terry Kelly states that "the importance of religion in the life of humanity stands: resilient throughout history; its deep appeal to the human psyche; its capacity to provide a guiding sense of ethics and morals; and its validation of mystical experiences of the 'other' that defy everyday explanations."[23]

THE IMAGE OF GOD

When most unbelievers reject God, it is often because of an image of God they hear about and see in action. That God can be worth rejecting. The theologian Marcus Borg says, "Tell me your image of God and I will tell you your theology."[24] The image of God some of us project is far removed from the merciful and loving Father that Jesus proclaimed. We need to be especially careful of believing so strongly in God's power and God's will that some of us end up proclaiming a God that sends evil. As I explored in much greater detail in *Where the Hell Is God?*, there is a big difference between God *permitting* evil in the world, which is complex enough, and God *sending evil* upon the world. We do not believe that God sends evil, for as John says, "God is light and in him there is no darkness at all" (1 John 1:5).

The 2003 film *Bruce Almighty* showcases the sort of obnoxious wonder-worker God that some Christians hold on to and to which atheists understandably reject. In the film, Bruce blames God for everything that goes wrong in his life—at home and at work. So God visits him and, since he thinks that he can do a better job of being God, he challenges him to have a go. He discovers it was more complex than he had anticipated. In fact, Steve Koren, Mark O'Keefe, and Steve Oedekerk's screenplay is theologically astute.[25]

God:	"You have all my powers. Use them any way you like. There are just two things you can't do: you can't tell anyone you're God. Believe me, you don't want that kind of attention."
Bruce:	"And the other?"
God:	"You can't mess with free will."
Bruce:	"Can I ask why?"
God:	"Yes you can! That's the beauty of it!"

Many Christians need to be reminded of the absolute centrality of the doctrine of free will. We are invited by God to cooperate with grace; we are never coerced.

At the end of the film, God says to Bruce, "The problem is that people keep looking up, when they should look inside....You want to see a miracle—then be a miracle." This film engagingly challenges us to get clear on our image of God, because sometimes what others reject is worth rejecting. God does not treat us like toys, sending terrible things to test us, to teach us something, or to get even. God did not kill Baron d'Holbach's wife. She died of an unknown illness in 1743 because we are finite, mortal beings, subject to disease and death.

CONCLUSION

Christian faith will not be judged by what we say as much as by what we do. As St. Francis of Assisi is reputed to have said, "Preach always and everywhere and if you must, use words." Imagine if all of the 2.2 billion Christians actually lived the faith, hope, and love we profess every day. That action alone might be enough evidence upon which to base a judgment that belief is an irresistible force for good.

Here is a personal story to illustrate my point:

During the long Christmas holidays when I was a seminarian, I worked in the pastoral care department of a big Catholic public hospital. At a Christmas party, I met the charge nurse of the maternity ward. Because I was a celibate, I pleaded that I would never be at a birth, and inquired if I might be allowed to attend one. The charge nurse thought that would be fine.

Weeks passed. Apparently, a student priest watching you have a baby is not the easiest thing to sell! Six weeks later I got the call. Mary (that was actually her name) was sixteen, had been dumped by her nineteen-year-old boyfriend, and shunned by her family. A kindly seminarian at the birth of her baby was obviously better than no one at all.

On my arrival on the ward, I did an "ante-natal class 101" in ten minutes:

- hold Mary's hand;
- don't get in the way;
- when the midwife tells Mary to "push and keep it coming, keep it coming, keep it coming, rest two, three, four, and breathe two, three, four, push, and keep it coming, keep it coming, keep it coming"— you say it too. (*If anyone wants to have a baby, as you can tell, I can help and can also do the baptism. Now that's value for money!*);
- finally, I was firmly told—don't faint!

Mary and I met six hours into her labor, which was an unusual circumstance within which to meet your "birthing partner." She had very little small talk, maybe because she had no breath at all. From my vast experience of childbirth, I thought everything was going along smoothly, until the doctor arrived to do an episiotomy. You don't want to know what that is, and I wish I didn't! I swear to God that analgesia would have been invented centuries earlier if men had to go through all of this. In fact, we would probably go on epidurals in the sixth month.

The baby arrived minutes later. Mary wept. She had very good cause to. I wept for no good reason, and the charge nurse wept because I was weeping. There is something so primal and human about the moment of birth that it bonds us to each other. Friendship born in the trenches took on a new meaning for me.

After the tears came the laughter and joy. The reality of Mary's tough situation was happily postponed.

On discharge, Mary asked me to baptize the baby. I couldn't, but I arranged for a priest friend to do it. I'm Benjamin Michael's godfather. I've stayed in touch with them for the last thirty years. Mary went on to have three more boys to three different fathers. Tommy, the third dad, is now her devoted husband.

When he was four, I got Benjamin into the local Catholic elementary school, where the principal was Sr. Mary Francis Xavier, a sister of St. Joseph. She was formidable but fair. She took an interest in Benjamin and his brothers. Only once did Sister have to go to Mary's home to demand that the boys get out of bed, were fed, cleaned, dressed, taken to school on time, and did their homework later. It paid off! Sister enrolled all the boys for scholarships at a Christian Brothers High School. On their own merits, each of them won a fully funded place and Sister wins a place in heaven.

Benjamin is a physiotherapist; Daniel is an accountant; Kai is a social worker; and Noah is a nurse. He has just finished his diploma in obstetrics.

Mary works at the local supermarket. Twenty years ago, I received her and her husband, Tommy, into the Catholic Church and married them. She now volunteers at the St. Vincent De Paul hostel for homeless women, where some of them are sixteen and pregnant.

From a complex conception, a messy birth, a willing midwife, and a vulnerable baby, extraordinary goodness has flowed from one generation to the next. The divine working through human hands at every stage has changed lives.

The best response to any aggressive atheist is not only to point out patiently the coherence in believing in something bigger than the here and now—in something more than what we can feel, touch, and see—but also to live what we believe, practice what we preach, and to do it with love and joy. Some people may never like the message, but it has a good effect on our lives, and the betterment of the world should itself be compelling evidence. We all know that when ideological fanatics use religion for their political ends, and when the worst criminal behaviors of a very few believers toward the most vulnerable members of society easily provide good reasons not to believe in any religion or God, then, with charity, we also need to ask what the world would be like without the best of religion. Would it be the panacea of rational humanity—some aggressive atheists argue it could be—or a meaningless life that would amount to a vacuous and hollow existence?

Chapter Two

QUESTIONS OF FAITH

While Tom and I were flying through the clouds and the mysteries of theology, an extraordinary array of questions and answers went back and forth between us. This process even has a name: the Socratic method, where questions and answers develop into a dialogue of critical thinking that leads to deeper questions and searching for more refined answers.

Tom had many questions, but in preparation for this chapter, I wrote to thirty young adult friends—believers and nonbelievers alike—and asked them to tell me the questions they most have or receive about the reasons for and against religious faith. I was especially interested in the young adults who had walked away from any belief in God or religion and the questions that saw them formally or informally depart. I thank all of them for their honesty and was struck by how many of them were easily collated or refined into one question or collected around a few themes. Hopefully, my summary and these all-too-brief answers assist a dialogue not just with the page, but in the real-life dialogues, where the search for meaning is so often pursued at depth.

ISN'T RELIGION THE CAUSE OF MOST WARS?

With the litany of wars that have been, or are, seemingly waged in the name of God(s) throughout history, the sense that religion is the primary cause of conflict in the world can easily be asserted. I don't want to let my coreligionists off the hook for the criminal acts and suffering they have perpetrated upon our sisters and brothers, but any careful analysis of almost all wars bears out that religion has not been the primary cause of most wars.

Certainly, religion has had and does have a role to play in the justification of war, and some shocking deeds have been done and are done in the name of God. However, Meic Pearse presents a more intelligent analysis of the causes of war in *The Gods of War: Is Religion the Primary Cause of Violent Conflict?*[1] Here, as well as in the highly respected *Encyclopedia of Wars*, we find that, tragically, there have been 1,763 official wars in all recorded human history. Pearse shows that believers have been responsible for sixty-eight religious wars. Pearse shows that the vast majority of the world's wars happen because of greed for land or resources, political power, and conflict over cultural, tribal, national, and social issues.

As far as Christianity is concerned, while we hold the theory of a just war, there should not have been any war conducted simply for religious ends. To justify their murderous behavior, leaders, including religious leaders, have evoked the greatest appeal to the highest authority they can—God. It is not by accident that an appeal to authority, simply on the basis of it being an authority, is a logical fallacy.

These days it is tragic and wrong that some Islamic ideologues talk about their deadly acts of terrorism as "holy wars." In the aftermath of 9/11, as we noted in the last chapter, the world's leading mainstream Islamic leaders condemned those attacks, and have subsequently condemned bin Laden, Al Qaeda, and other Islamic terrorist groups as the equivalent of war criminals whose desires do not represent Muslims and whose actions are incompatible with Islam. There are approximately 1.6 billion Muslims in the world, the vast majority of whom live by the often-quoted teaching in the Qur'an: "If any one slew a person… it would be as if he slew the whole people: and if any one saved a life, it would be as if he saved the life of the whole people" (Surat Al-Mā'idah 5:32).

The reality is that religion, as one among many tools, has been and is sometimes used in political, social, and ethnic wars, in the false search for social and political uniformity and colonial dominance. Furthermore, apart from war and even more tragically, religion has mounted its own persecutions.

I do not want to run away from the despicable fallout from the 595-year reign of the "inquisitors of heretical depravity." It is impossible to know how many people were actually killed in this period by these theological tyrants, but most reputable scholars on the Inquisition conclude that it was somewhere between three and five thousand people. Not one person should have been murdered for who they were (homosexuals), for what they did (notorious sinners and so-called witches), and for what they believed (atheists, Jews, and Muslims). Having now formally apologized for the Inquisition (easy in hindsight), I have no knowledge of the Catholic Church sanctioning the death of anyone since 1826, which is more than we can say for every other nation or state on earth.

Humanity does not need religion to be murderous. A horrible statistic to know is that the atheistic regimes of the Soviet Union, Communist China, the Nazis, Pol Pot, and other nationalist regimes accounted for 1.2 billion deaths in the twentieth century. Some atheists object to believers saying this. Sam Harris: "People of faith often claim that the crimes of Hitler, Stalin, Mao and Pol Pot were the inevitable product of unbelief. The problem is that they are too much like religions. Such regimes are dogmatic to the core and generally give rise to personality cults that are indistinguishable from cults of religious hero worship....There is no society in human history that ever suffered because its people became too reasonable."[2]

That these murderous regimes and their evil output were *inevitable* products of their unbelief is unconvincing. However, these regimes were atheistic in word and deed, and mounted the largest scale and most systematic murder of innocents the world has ever known. Clifford Geertz once famously defined religion as "a system of symbols, which acts to establish powerful, pervasive and long-lasting moods and motivations in men [*sic*], by formulating conceptions of a general order of existence and, clothing these conceptions with such an aura of factuality that the moods and motivations seem uniquely realistic."[3] Given this, we can see some validity in Harris's argument in regard to the symbolic presentations of communism, fascism, and Nazism, but the same could also be applied to some families, sporting clubs, and social institutions that have elaborate quasi-religious rituals. Just because a state or group borrows and adapts religious-style myths and rituals, that does not lead to murderous behavior, nor does it mean that religions inevitably murder because of their myths and rituals. Harris seems to be arguing that if the world had his brand of atheism—against those other murderous brands—we would not have any murder.

The sad reality is that in human conflict, especially when it involves greed for land or resources, political power, and conflict over cultural, tribal, national, and social issues, religion is one of the many things used to uphold the rightness of the claim and the justification for war. However, it is simply not true to say that Christianity and religion has been the cause and effect of most wars in the world.

DOES THE QUR'AN INSIST ON VIOLENT AGGRESSION?

We need to be upfront but clear about the present issues regarding Islam. The distinguished journalist, Fareed Zakaria, born into an Islamic family, neatly sums up the grave issues here:

> But let's be honest. Islam has a problem today. The places that have trouble accommodating themselves to the modern world are disproportionately Muslim. In 2013, of the top 10 groups that perpetrated terrorist attacks, seven were Muslim. Of the top 10 countries where terrorist attacks took place, seven were Muslim-majority. The Pew Research Center rates countries on the level of restrictions that governments impose on the free exercise of religion. Of the 24 most restrictive

countries, 19 are Muslim-majority. Of the 21 countries that have laws against apostasy, all have Muslim majorities. There is a cancer of extremism within Islam today. A small minority of Muslims celebrates violence and intolerance and harbors deeply reactionary attitudes toward women and minorities. While some confront these extremists, not enough do so, and the protests are not loud enough. How many mass rallies have been held against the Islamic State (also known as ISIS) in the Arab world today?[4]

Although this book refers primarily to Christianity, this question about Islam is too important not to explore. Since the rise of radical Islam, some people have tried to claim that Islam is inherently and violently expansionist. Like Christianity, and unlike Judaism, Islam is a proselytizing religion. We both seek converts. Just as Christianity, as noted, has been regularly and appallingly marshaled to justify war and colonization, "for God, king, and country," the same rhetoric is being used by radical and criminal terrorists, who scandalously claim Islam as their motivation and justification.

Nothing in any religion, anywhere and anytime, justifies violent conversion. As already noted, when the separation of church and state becomes blurred, theology and political ideology become tragic partners in state-sanctioned murder. Mehdi Hasan, a Muslim journalist, has shown that the Western world is not fighting Islam, we are fighting terrorism, and that even some of the leading so-called jihadists purchased *Islam for Dummies* and *The Koran for Dummies* before setting off on their murderous tour of duty in God's name. That's how deeply steeped in Islam they are. For many of these political radicals, religion is reduced to slogans.

Hasan observes, "In 2008, a classified briefing note on radicalization, prepared by MI5's behavioural science unit, was leaked to the *Guardian*. It revealed that, 'far from being religious zealots, a large number of those involved in terrorism do not practise their faith regularly. Many lack religious literacy and could... be regarded as religious novices.' The analysts concluded that 'a well-established religious identity actually protects against violent radicalization.'"[5] As Hasan concludes, what motivates radical terrorists has more to do with poverty, moral outrage, disaffection, peer pressure, and the search for a new identity and sense of belonging and purpose. Any serious research of the backgrounds of the individuals whom we know have been involved in the so-called Islamic holy wars indicates that they appear to have serious mental health issues and that their religion, which they very often do not practice, is distorted by their undiagnosed and untreated pathology: "Long beards and flowing robes aren't indicators of radicalization; ultra-conservative or reactionary views don't automatically lead to violent acts. Muslims aren't all Islamists, Islamists aren't all jihadists and jihadists aren't all devout. To claim otherwise isn't only factually inaccurate; it could be fatal."

Sadly, even intelligent people—some who should know better—can make erroneous statements. For example, John Stackhouse, the distinguished Professor of Theology and Culture at Regent College, Vancouver, claimed,

> Islam is not a religion of peace. They've tried to trademark that but it's just not true. Islam is a religion that copes with the real world and in Islam, including in its holy books, there are provisions for warfare and there are provisions for defensive warfare and there are also provisions for the extension of Islam, which is why the whole history of Islam has been steady territorial expansion. Of course it's a religion of peace, by which they mean the subjugation of other people under sharia and that's peace but it is an imperial sort of peace and I'm not judging it. I mean, we Christians have done the same thing and lots of other religions have done the same thing as well....I mean, as a matter of fact, the Qur'an and the sharia are very clear

that the jihad can be both the internal, the greater jihad of subjecting myself to the will of God, and the lesser jihad is to subject the world to God....While many of my Muslim friends...have no interest in the violent prosecution of their faith...I think it's really important to understand, nonetheless, we just can't make sense of world history if we suggest that Islam doesn't have within it the legitimation of violence.[6]

There are several problems here. We have observed how wrong it is to talk as though there is one type of Christianity, or one type of atheism. The same is true of saying "Islam is...". It does not make sense. This also applies to whether one says, "Islam is a religion of peace" or "Islam is a religion of expansionist violence." The reality is that the vast majority of the 1.6 billion Muslims in the world peacefully coexist with their neighbors, and their religion gives them resources to achieve this peaceful coexistence.

It can also be claimed that some texts in the Qur'an *can* be interpreted—not *have* to be interpreted—as permitting or even commanding warfare. For example: "And when the sacred months have passed, then kill the polytheists wherever you find them and capture them and besiege them and sit in wait for them at every place of ambush. But if they should repent, establish prayer, and give zakah, let them [go] on their way. Indeed, Allah is Forgiving and Merciful" (Qur'an, Surat At-Tawbah 9:5). The Muslim tradition has ways of interpreting these texts according to what seems appropriate to people at the time. It always comes down to how we interpret texts—religious, political, social, cultural, or educational.

Most Muslims would interpret Surat 9:5 as referring to Muhammad in Medina in the seventh century and its expansion into what was the then-decaying Roman Empire. In fact, most of Islam's territorial expansion was not through conquest but by the preaching of Sufis. So it is not hard to read these violent texts in their historical context and interpret the whole tradition in peaceful ways. Otherwise one will need to argue that one-fifth of the human race cannot live at peace and that ISIS and radical Muslims are the "real Muslims," even though these men are primarily killing other Muslims.

Furthermore, Christians and Jews have to be very careful because the commentary that violent Islamic texts can *only* be interpreted literally by Muslims today can fall back on us as well. God's call for and delight in the genocide of the Amalekites in 1 Samuel 15:1–3 is one that comes to mind, but there are many others, including the great flood in Genesis 6, the destruction of Sodom and Gomorrah in Genesis 19, and the destruction of Jericho in Joshua 6, just to name a few, where God's desire for his way of life to be believed and lived by all leads to violent retribution against the guilty and the innocent alike.

Furthermore, there are many atheists who argue that the violent texts in the New Testament prove that Christianity is, in fact, a violent religion. In Matthew 5:17–19, Jesus teaches that everyone will be subject to his commandments, even though we are not told how that will happen, though in Luke 19:27 Jesus says, "But as for these enemies of mine who did not want me to be king over them—bring them here and slaughter them in my presence." And there is no question that a literal reading of the stories in regard to the end of time are fairly violent for unbelievers, filled as they are with unquenchable fires, weeping and gnashing of teeth, the eternal torment of hell, and with wars, famines, and disease.

However, most intelligent and educated Jews and Christians no longer read these texts as discourses literally, but rather in their context, within their time and community. We have also left behind selling our daughters into slavery (Exod 21:7), or buying slaves from neighboring nations (Lev 25:44), having no contact with a woman while she is having her menstrual cycle (Lev 15:19–24), killing a neighbor who insists on working on the Sabbath (Exod 35:2), eating shellfish (Lev 11:10), approaching the altar of God if there is a defect in our sight (Lev 21:20), killing a man who has a haircut (Lev 19:27), farming two crops at any one time (Lev 19:19), stoning someone who curses or uses the Lord's name in vain (Lev 24:10–16), and burning anyone to death who commits adultery with an in-law (Lev 20:14). Furthermore, most sane Christians are not actually cutting off hands or plucking out eyes that may cause them to sin (Matt 5:29), and to my knowledge, we never put someone to death who cursed their parents (Matt 15:4–7), or destroyed entire towns that do not receive the Gospel (Luke 10:10–15), and we are not wrangling snakes or scorpions or drinking poison to prove that we are good Christians (Mark 16:17–18).

Despite what some atheists say and what the enemies of Islam argue, religions change and develop and evolve. The believers interpret their sacred texts in the light of tools at their disposal in order to understand their own history; they discern the essentials of their faith from those texts that refer to a time and period that has passed, and take into account the contemporary setting in living the faith. All religions have some way to go in this regard, but the intelligent and common sense majority should not be summarily condemned along with the distorted ideology that can emerge from the most unwell, ignorant, or criminal religious minority.

HOW DO WE MAINTAIN OUR FAITH WHEN CLERGY HAVE ABUSED CHILDREN SEXUALLY, AND THEN CHURCH LEADERS HAVE COVERED UP THEIR ACTIONS?

In the last twenty years, I cannot recall a serious conversation about the validity of religion where this issue has not been raised. This issue has a personal edge for me. Since being ordained in 1993, I have seriously questioned my vocation on three occasions, and each time the questioning emerged out of revelations about the crimes of clergy against minors and the cover-up of those crimes by church officials.

There is no question that this criminal behavior has been one of the greatest moments of evil, both in the abuse itself, and in its cover-up. Having established a Papal Commission for Protecting Minors from Clerical Sex Abuse, Pope Francis stated, "We must go ahead with zero tolerance. A priest who has sex with a child betrays God. A priest needs to lead children to sanctity, and children trust him. But instead he abuses them, and this is terrible."

Then, in his meeting with survivors of clerical abuse on Monday, July 7, 2014, he said even more clearly,

> There is no place in the Church's ministry for those who commit these abuses, and I commit myself not to tolerate harm done to a minor by any individual, whether a cleric or not. All bishops must carry out their pastoral ministry with the utmost care in order to help foster the protection of minors, and they will be held accountable....I ask (your) support so as to help me ensure that we develop better policies and procedures in the universal Church for the protection of minors and for the training of church personnel in implementing those policies and procedures. We need to do everything in our power to ensure that these sins have no place in the Church....(May God) give us the grace to be ashamed.[7]

For those of us who have met survivors of clerical sexual abuse of minors, and the secondary victims, their families, we know that no apology can ever repair the damage, no amount of compensation can give someone back their innocence and childhood, and no act of reparation or penance can ever adequately express the shame and sorrow of what all of us feel over what a very few clergy have done.

That said, along with many other Catholics whom I know, I hope, first, that all church officials, against whom credible allegations of child abuse have been upheld, will be dismissed from the priesthood and the religious life. No matter when it was committed, the sexual abuse of a child nullifies any commitment to the priesthood or belonging to a religious order. It is, for many believers, the line in the sand. Christian forgiveness starts with holding people accountable for what they have done, and it has consequences. No one is beyond God's mercy and forgiveness; however, some actions by a very few church officials prevent them from continuing to be leaders.

Second, if the survivors wish to go to the police, the Church should support them in their decision, be transparent in the legal process, and hand over the alleged perpetrator for secular legal investigation. Third, if the survivors do not wish to pursue a legal remedy, the Church needs to establish the truth of their claims through an independent conciliation, arbitration, and compensation process. Fourth, officials who have covered up these crimes should be subjected to civil and ecclesiastical penalties. Finally, if the pursuit of justice means that the Church needs to sell property and liquidate assets to settle just claims with survivors, then the Church should recognize that people always matter more than land and buildings. Though no cash can ever repair the damage, it is one indication of the seriousness of action in the face of our newfound rhetoric.

There are, however, four other related issues in this conversation. First, without justifying one case, clergy are not the only people to have abused a child and church officials are not the only ones to cover it up. In every OECD country, the most common place for a child to be abused is in the family home with a person known to the family. In most of these countries, that rate has hovered around 83 percent of all cases for over two decades. While it is true that religious officials who preach social and personal morality should be held to a higher standard than most, it would be a rare individual who would argue that expectations in regard to a child's family should be any less than in religious organizations. Because we know that prosecution rates of family abusers do not follow anything like these consistent statistics, then we can conclude that a tremendous number of families also know about covering up this crime.

Second, credibility demands that we are consistent on the question of child sexual abuse and child protection, so, no matter when it was committed, child sexual abuse in a family must be reported to the police and the alleged perpetrator handed over for investigation. If the victim does not wish to pursue a legal remedy, there must be an independent conciliation, arbitration, and compensation process for them to access. The family may need to come to a just settlement with the victim. Any member of the family who has covered up these crimes should also be subjected to civil penalties as well.

It is perfectly understandable why it is easier for some people to get angry with churches in regard to sexual abuse of children. However, it is fair to acknowledge that, seeing this crime as a moral failure—one that could be changed when challenged—it did not have to be reported to the police even though laws specifically forbidding child sexual abuse emerged in most OECD countries in the 1960s and 1970s (yes, incredibly, they are that late). Tragically and tellingly, child sexual abuse can be found wherever there is access, power, and pathology. To be ruthlessly consistent, which I assume all people of good will want to be in regard to child protection issues, we should soon see active and retired government officials, school leaders, sporting coaches and college presidents, retired and serving officers in the defense forces, Scouts, officials of every other major Christian denomination, and other religious groups be equally scrutinized, charged, and convicted for the crimes and the cover-up of the crimes.

Third, while I long to see a change to the discipline of mandatory celibacy for Catholic diocesan priests, I do not want it to be done because of child sexual abuse. There can be little doubt that in some cases celibacy has been a disaster in the psycho-sexual maturity of some individuals, and most studies do find that celibate priests commit abuse at a higher rate than the population as a whole, and in comparison to married men. However, the same studies also point to other factors like access and power.

From personal experience, celibacy also enshrines a class or caste system in the Catholic Church that can be secretive, unaccountable, unassailable, and doesn't have to answer to secular community standards, valuations, and expectations. As in most things, celibacy can be a life-giving gift of oneself for the betterment of humanity, but it can also be a force for personal and communal destruction. Therefore, I welcome a change in the discipline of celibacy for diocesan priests, but prefer that we do not do it in response to child protection issues because that will not solve the problem.

Finally, it is often claimed that the place where clergy are most protected is in the Catholic confessional. Ever since Hitchcock's 1953 film, *I Confess*, the public has seen this moment as potentially sinister. Priests break the "seal of confession" if in any way the identity of the penitent is exposed, but we are able to talk about "cases," in exactly the same way lawyers or doctors can do so. More generally, I have never heard the confession of anyone admitting to child sexual abuse. I have asked at least a hundred others priests of varying ages if they ever heard the confession of a pedophile priest. None have and I believe them. So, while it is possible, and even looks accommodating for the Church to give them a veil of secrecy in the confessional, it would be extremely rare for a child abuser who needs silence to do his evil actions to take the risk of telling anyone about what he has done. We also know that pedophiles lead psychologically compartmentalized lives, so while the general public thinks that child-abusing priests, for example, must need to repent of their crimes to function, psychological and family studies tell us that perpetrators do not process these actions in the same way the rest of us do and that, as difficult as it is for anyone of us to accept, these criminals can abuse children and carry on with their daily lives as though no crime has been committed.

To my knowledge, there are only two vocations whose professional disclosures are presently protected by the courts: lawyers and priests. Medicos used to be, but, now, they must mandatorily report any child sexual abuse. (I have often wondered how psychiatrists cope with that one.) However, the nature of the conversations of lawyers and priests has been recognized as having qualities that the law deems should be protected, and these are related.

If a person is to be defended, the lawyers need to know the truth, even if some of the truth they hear is criminal. The lawyers need the whole story. If a penitent is to repent, then he or she needs to be able to tell the truth. The priest should hear the whole story. If we now make the priest liable for what he hears in confession, then I assume we will also make lawyers liable for what they hear from clients in conference. No exceptions.

In any case, in the extremely unlikely event that someone came to me to confess the sin of child sexual abuse, it does not mean that they are automatically forgiven by God or the Church. To fulfill all the obligations of the sacrament, child predators have to be sorry for their sins, have a sincere purpose to amend their lives (stop the crimes), and as an expression of this, they must do their penance. I would make absolution contingent on that penitent and I calling or going to the police immediately—right there and then. No penance, no absolution. This is, clearly, not foolproof, and more seriously, it is not right in the face of the crime, but I could not imagine perpetrators, actually and genuinely coming to the sacrament of penance and confessing this egregious sin, who have no desire to take responsibility for what they had done to their victims and allow me to accompany them to the authorities.

For consistency, I often wonder if those who are interested in the confessional seal would also want priests to report other illegal behavior we may hear such as drug use; any type of theft; any physical or sexual abuse of adults—especially rape in marriage; some forms of pornography; avoidance of taxation; software piracy; hastening death or assisting a suicide; and the failure of anyone to report a crime to the police. It was not long ago that it would have also meant reporting a woman who had an abortion. Given the civil law in some countries currently, it would also mean that Catholic priests would have to report adultery and homosexuality to the police. Some of our detractors want to spend a lot of time and energy on this issue in regard to child sexual abuse in the Church, and while it is an interesting conversation to have, the actual experience of priests in the confessional bears out the truth of the old ethical line: *extreme cases don't prove principles*.

IS THE BIBLE TRUE? HOW CAN PEOPLE BASE THEIR BELIEF ON A BOOK FILLED WITH CONTRADICTIONS, INCORRECT SCIENCE, AND TIME-BOUND CUSTOMS?

When I began studying for the priesthood, seminarians were told that at some stage in our formation we would have to spend a year addressing our personal issues professionally with a psychiatrist so that, potentially, we would not lump them on to others in the future. Many of my contemporaries resented this requirement as an imposition. I am not sure what it says about me, but I loved it! Someone was going to be paid to listen to me each week for a whole year. Mind you, my psychiatrist went to sleep on me four times that year. That's how exciting my psyche was. In fact, I thought I should invent things just to keep my shrink awake!

Of all the wonderful observations this psychiatrist made to me that year, among one of his best was, "I know when someone has moved from adolescence to adulthood because they are not emotionally all or nothing." As an example, he told me about a fifteen-year-old girl who asks her parents for permission to go to a local dance. "We would be delighted for that, darling," says Dad, "but your mother and I want you home by 10:30 p.m." With a big pout, his adolescent daughter replies, "Well I'm not going, then. If I can't stay out until midnight like everyone else, then I won't go." She doesn't go. For most adolescents, life is reduced to all or nothing, black or white, it's true or false. I know a good many fifty-year-olds who are only fifteen years of age emotionally.

This advice is helpful in approaching the Bible. Many young and not so young adults, believers and unbelievers alike, want the Bible to be either all true or all false. This position is theologically adolescent. The Bible is, literally, a library of books of varying relevance, importance, and application. Though we can enter into its riches on many levels, to get the most out of it, we need to pay careful attention to it as a literary text, its history, the time and circumstance of its writing, the community that produced it, the way it reflects its culture, and the larger religious messages that emerge from it. Any one part of a particular book, and any one book within the Bible, needs to be read against the wider message of the Bible as a whole. This is especially true for Christians as we read parts of the Old Testament.

Until the late nineteenth century, the vast majority of Christians read the Bible literally. Even though it sometimes contradicted itself, it was the Word of God, and so every detail in it had to be factually true. This position always had problems. For instance, there is not just one creation story—the famous seven-day version in Genesis 1. In Genesis 2, we have another creation story where we are not told how long creation took, but it seems to happen very quickly, and it occurs in a completely different order from Genesis 1. In this second creation account, the garden is not perfect but a place of work, wherein some spaces are already dangerous and off-limits. Lesser known creation stories come later in Psalm 104 and Job 38, where God just places the earth on its axis on the sea. Then in Psalm 74, we are told that God creates the order of the world by first slaying the chaos created by sea monsters. The Bible's cosmology looks like this:

- the earth was flat, motionless, and sitting serenely at the center of a simple three-layered universe with heaven above and hell below;
- the sun, moon, stars, and other heavenly bodies circled a stationary earth;
- the flat earth rested on pillars;
- the moon emitted light;
- the universe was composed of water; and
- rain occurred when God opened up windows in the sky.

If we are looking for science here, we are in trouble. It cannot all be factual, and none of it is. It is the best a prescientific people could do to explain the created order. They did their best with what they had.

For over a century, Christians have been working hard to understand the Bible's theology, history, literature, culture, context, and the communities that produced each of the books in the biblical library. Though many of us were taught otherwise by well-meaning preachers and teachers, for the last fifty years the Catholic Church has taught that the Bible is not to be interpreted literally.

Nevertheless, we are not theologically adolescent. We are not all or nothing. The Bible is not just all right or all wrong. Bernard Lonergan, SJ, has offered a very helpful contribution in this debate. Lonergan makes a distinction between truth and fact.[8] Although there are facts in the Bible, it was not written, nor should it be interpreted, as a book of facts. It was written as stories, historical accounts, wisdom, poetry, prophecies, letters, parables, and apocalyptic literature to evoke images, emotions, and responses to the religious truths it is expounding. So the Bible is a library of books, of varying relevance and importance, containing religious truths. The Catholic Church believes the Bible cannot err in revealing to us what we need to know for our salvation, notably God's saving love and mercy.

As Christians, of course, we believe that Jesus is the definitive revelation of God for the world, so we have to approach all revelation in the Old Testament through the prism of Christ. As Christians, we believe that if there is a conflict between the image of God that emerges between some parts of the Old Testament and the definitive revelation of God in Jesus Christ, then we go for Jesus. It concerns me that some people think we have a split-personality God: nasty God the Father in heaven who kills and maims and inflicts plagues upon creation; loving Jesus; and the bird-like Spirit who hovers around and abides with us still. But we do not believe this. The Father and Son and Spirit are three personae of the one, same God. St. John of Damascus said the Trinity was a dance, a

Pas de trois. St. Ignatius Loyola described it as three notes in a single chord. St. Patrick famously used the three-leaf clover as a teaching aid to get the point across to the Irish, and St. Augustine thought the Trinity acted in unison in the same way that memory, intelligence, and will does within each of us.

Not being a Jew, I can let go of the way the Hebrews interpreted the presence and action of God in various events of their history because some images are completely irreconcilable with the person and work of Christ. I can see why Richard Dawkins could say, "The God of the Old Testament is arguably the most unpleasant character in all fiction: jealous and proud of it; a petty, unjust, unforgiving control-freak; a vindictive, bloodthirsty ethnic cleanser; a misogynistic, homophobic, racist, infanticidal, genocidal, filicidal, pestilential, megalomaniacal, sadomasochistic, capriciously malevolent bully."[9] Conveniently, what Dawkins does not say in his selective caricature is that there are many more instances in the Old Testament where God is also presented as loving, forgiving, gentle, compassionate, just, merciful, faithful, and joyous.

When it comes to Jesus, however, there is not a single moment in the New Testament when Jesus is petty, unjust, an unforgiving control freak, vindictive, a bloodthirsty ethnic cleanser, a misogynist, homophobic, racist, infanticidal, genocidal, filicidal, pestilential, megalomaniacal, sadomasochistic, or a capriciously malevolent bully.

Don't turn the cleansing of the temple in John 2, for example, into a frenzy of bloody violence. In this scene, which is in all four Gospels, Jesus becomes angry at the unjust exploitation of the poor in God's name. It is only in John that we are told, in the Greek text, that with uncharacteristic anger, he "made a whip from cords," not a Roman scourge, and he sent the money changers scurrying.

The idea that Jesus corrects as well as fulfills the Old Testament for Christians is not some new trendy Christian theology. As John records,

If you know me, you will know my Father also. From now on you do know him and have seen him....Whoever has seen me has seen the Father....The words that I say to you I do not speak on my own; but the Father who dwells in me does his works. Believe me that I am in the Father and the Father is in me...and the word that you hear is not mine, but is from the Father who sent me. (John 14:7–11, 24)

This is why Christians intermittently left behind animal sacrifices, selling our children into slavery, infanticide, mandatory circumcision, killing anyone who works on the Sabbath, and declaring that pigs, camels, carnivorous birds, sea creatures without fins and scales, most insects, rodents, and reptiles were unclean and could not be eaten.

It is true that first-century Christians did not leave everything behind, some of which we now wish they had. It took Christians centuries to see the inhumanity of slavery, and this includes Pope Nicholas V's shameful 1452 decree that Catholic nations had the right to enslave non-Christians. However, it was also devout Christians like William Wilberforce from 1785, and Charles Spurgeon, John Wesley, Charles Finney, Theodore Weld, George Bourne, George B. Cheever, Pope Benedict XIV in 1741, Pius VII in 1815, Daniel O'Connell and the Quaker abolitionists, Benjamin Lay, and John Woolman who, along with many great secularists in these centuries, vigorously denounced slavery and agitated for an end to this evil.

Similarly, there is no question that Christian thinking on the role and leadership of women is going through a similar and welcome development. It is equally true that science is rightly and presently challenging the biblical presumptions behind the nature and nurture debate in regard to homosexuality. It is important to note here, again, that while Jesus has next to nothing to say about human sexuality in the Gospels, he has much to say about the dignity of all people, the command to love oneself, and of the universal call to be compassionate.

So letting go of some of the time-bound customs in the Bible is a work in progress for all Christians, informed now by the best of biblical studies, modern psychology, science, and philosophy. As "people of the Book," we are not frightened of the contemporary world; we use it to enable us to illuminate the central truths within the biblical library that is read in the light of the teaching of Jesus, so we can live our salvation here and now.

IS THERE ANY EVIDENCE THAT JESUS ACTUALLY LIVED, AND EVEN IF HE DID, ISN'T HIS STORY JUST A RELIGIOUS VERSION OF THE SUPERMAN STORY?

There are some who argue that Jesus is a historical invention, but they are in the vast minority of opinion, scholarly or otherwise. It is true that the earliest written evidence of Jesus is found in the New Testament, which clearly has a stake in the story! Though the order is debated, the first six writings are generally agreed to be James, dating from around AD 50; 1 Thessalonians (52—53); 2 Thessalonians (52—53); Galatians (55); 1 Corinthians (57); and 2 Corinthians (57—58). Given that Jesus most probably died in Jerusalem between AD 34 and 36, the first written material about Jesus comes sixteen to twenty-two years after he lived, probably because the first eyewitnesses to his life were dying.

We also have two other nonbiblical sources. In his *Antiquities of the Jews* (c. AD 93), Jewish historian Josephus tells us that Jesus was crucified on the orders of Pontius Pilate. In the *Annals* (c. AD 116), the Roman historian Tacitus also records that Pilate crucified Jesus.

Rather than citing instances of a man called Jesus, however, maybe the many references to the earliest followers of Jesus are equally telling. Explaining why Nero blamed the Christians for the fire of Rome in AD 64, Tacitus writes, "Nero fastened the guilt…on a class hated for their abominations, called Christians by the populace. Christus, from whom the name had its origin, suffered the extreme penalty during the reign of Tiberius at the hands of…Pontius Pilatus, and a most mischievous superstition, thus checked for the moment, again broke out not only in Judaea, the first source of the evil, but even in Rome" (*Annals* 15.44).

In AD 112, Pliny the Younger writes to Emperor Trajan about if and how he should prosecute the "great many" cases against people accused of being Christians:

> They were in the habit of meeting on a certain fixed day before it was light, when they sang in alternate verses a hymn to Christ, as to a god, and bound themselves by a solemn oath, not to any wicked deeds, but never to commit any fraud, theft or adultery, never to falsify their word, nor deny a trust when they should be called upon to deliver it up; after which it was their custom to separate, and then reassemble to partake of food—but food of an ordinary and innocent kind.[10]

There are also passing references to Jesus and Christians in the earlier writings in the Babylonian Talmud, a collection of Jewish rabbinical writings from AD 70 to 200. Lucian of Samosata, a Greek satirist, wrote in *The Death of Peregrine* (AD 165–75) that "the Christians...worship a man to this day—the distinguished personage who introduced their novel rites, and was crucified on that account....[It] was impressed on them by their original lawgiver that they are all brothers, from the moment that they are converted, and deny the gods of Greece, and worship the crucified sage, and live after his laws."[11]

However, even more striking proof comes from actions rather than words. Apart from the New Testament, where we hear about Saul murdering Stephen for his faith in Jesus, and the martyrdom of James, son of Zebedee, Josephus documents the martyrdom of James the Just. And from their own documents we know the Roman's first systematic, as against local, persecution of Christians began in Rome in AD 64. Therefore, about thirty-four to thirty-six years after Jesus had died, the emperor Nero decreed that Christianity was punishable by death. Anyone who would not offer sacrifice to the Roman gods could be and was often killed by the state. Later Christians claimed that it was during this time that Peter was martyred.

A century later, there are Roman records of Justin Martyr and his six fellow Christians going on trial and being executed in AD 164. The later reigns of Emperors Decius, Diocletian, and Galerius were especially bloody for Christians. In all of this, the earliest and later Christians were not giving their lives for a phantom, an idea, or a cause. They were giving their lives in following Jesus, the one they called the Christ.

Insofar as we can establish for certain that the then-secondary figures of the ancient world lived, we know that a man called Jesus from Nazareth lived and died in Palestine in the first part of the first century. The second part of the question, however, moves from the historical evidence and probabilities that we can muster, to the claims made about Jesus by Christians. Given my different perspective, it is understandable why some younger people might dismiss Christ as a religious version of the Superman story.

First, historically, superheroes are not a new phenomenon. Greek and Roman religions had pantheons of gods with superpowers. The present superheroes owe a debt to this pagan heritage. The entire premise of most of the superheroes in Greek philosophy and literature is that of the good vigilante, where someone restores moral good. It was Aristotle who said, "There are men, so godlike, so exceptional, that they naturally, by right of their extraordinary gifts, transcend all moral judgment or constitutional control: 'There is no law which embraces men of that caliber: they are themselves law.'"[12]

The modern superhero tradition, including Superman, emerged from this tradition as well, in nineteenth-century Victorian and Edwardian novels. Robin Hood and the Scarlet Pimpernel were the earliest adventurers, followed by Zorro and Tarzan, to name but two of the more famous. Then in the 1930s, four of the most popular superheroes were invented: the Shadow, Hercules, Spiderman, and Superman.

There are common traits between the ancient and the more

recent incarnations of the superhero: extraordinary powers and abilities; special weapons or devices (e.g., lasso, shield, webbing, hammer, or staff); a strong moral code in the service of the greater good; no expectation of reward; a refusal, or a dislike, to kill; being especially called to the role as vocation; their real identity is a secret; they have a distinctive dress; a core symbol expresses their presence, whether they are physically present or not (a bat, a star, a cape); though they have at least one or two devoted followers, they work independently, and are often misunderstood, especially by authority; they have identifiable enemies; they have supporters who assist in their mission; they have an incredible story of origin, which bestows on them the responsibility of their vocation, and their public reception is often mixed.

The problem with arguing that Jesus is like Superman is that the more persuasive argument is exactly the other way around. Apart from sharing many of the traits above, there are more direct similarities between Superman and Jesus: both are sent by their father to save the earth; when the time comes for their work to begin, both at thirty, Jesus goes to the desert and Superman goes to the artic wilderness; both confront evil and seek to destroy its hold on the world; both are stabbed in the side—one with Kryptonite, the other with a spear; and Jesus is lifted up on a cross while Superman flies in same pose. Many of the recent superhero creations are all secular presentations of Christian theology about Jesus Christ.

That said, I do not want to play down two things about Jesus that some Christians want to ignore or don't know. He is not the only religious figure where his followers accept that he had an extraordinary birth story. Religious founders like Zoroaster, Buddha, and Krishna are all immaculately conceived. Great men of their day like Pythagoras, Plato, Alexander, and Augustus are also said to have had an extraordinary birth narrative.

Equally, while some claim that there are many "crucified messiahs" in history, these claims are strongly contested between secular and Christian scholars, especially the bogus Horus/Jesus comparison. There are, however, other mythologies where a god dies and rises again: Osiris, Adonis, Attis, and Marduk are four that can be academically established.

Given that our Christian belief about Jesus' origins, death, and resurrection are matters for faith, they cannot be scientifically proved or disproved. In any case, other examples of similar claims in other mythologies and religions show that the ancient world saw the singularity and prominence of the person through these elements within the narrative.

What we do know is that within a decade of Jesus' life, death, and resurrection, Christianity is found in nearly every major center in the eastern Roman Empire: Jerusalem, Antioch, Ephesus, Corinth, Thessalonica, Cyprus, Crete, and Rome. It spread like wildfire. Why? Whatever else happened after the death of Jesus, something so powerful was unleashed that, among others, uneducated Galilean fishermen, together with the Pharisee and Roman citizen Saul/Paul, were so emboldened by their experience of Jesus that they took on the might of the Roman Empire, and like generations after them, were prepared to pay the price of following him even to the point of dying for him. Very few people will die for nothing. Something had happened to them all. No one to my knowledge has died for Superman.

HOW COULD A GOOD AND LOVING GOD NEED OR WANT JESUS TO SUFFER AND DIE ON GOOD FRIDAY?

There is hardly a more debated area of theology than what Protestants call "satisfaction theology" and Catholics call "atonement theory." Though the emphasis is different for both groups, these ideas wrestle with why Jesus died on Good Friday, and what role a loving God had in it.

It was noted earlier that until the last hundred years the entire Christian tradition read the Bible literally. This is no one's fault. In the wake of science challenging biblical ideas in the Enlightenment, the nineteenth century saw the coming together of rationalist philosophy, advances in comparative literature and languages, archaeology, and historical methods that were then applied to the texts, contexts, sources, forms, and literary styles of the books in the Bible. Furthermore, throughout the twentieth century, science was able to propose and debate coherent theories about how the earth and humanity evolved. However, this meant that previous thinking in regard to the literal truth of the Book of Genesis had to be revisited.

The traditional understanding of why Jesus died is entirely dependent on a literal reading of Genesis chapter 2, where humanity's original parents, Adam and Eve, offended God by eating of the fruit of the tree of knowledge, in an attempt to establish themselves as god, knowing good and evil. This triggers a series of events: loss of innocence, hiding from God, blaming each other for the action, the serpent condemned as the embodiment of evil, women suffering in childbirth, and later, Adam and Eve expelled from Eden, the place of paradise. The reverse side of Adam and Eve's original sin is the alienation it established between the perfect Creator and his imperfect creatures, and his subsequent lament and anger at humanity's fall into sinfulness. We now read these chapters as the Hebrews theologizing about how evil came into the world, why human beings are imperfect and sin, and about our estrangement from God.

Once the breach between heaven and earth had begun, the rest of the Old Testament could be fairly described as God wrestling with his chosen people to bring about a healing of the breach. Israel longs and hopes and looks for the day when such a remarriage between heaven and earth can occur.

As Israel keeps reflecting on how reconciliation might be effected, a central metaphor becomes the years during which the Israelites wandered in the desert. The Messiah, the anointed one, would be the one who would bring them home. Though there are several expectations of the Messiah in the Old Testament, it was generally thought that he would restore Israel either politically, ethically, or ritually. In Isaiah 53, we hear that this suffering servant will also be wounded for the sins of humanity and be the offering to God as an innocent scapegoat for all, or as a spotless lamb, offered on behalf of humanity, so that through him God's reign of justice and peace would be established.

Israel adopted a transactional model to explain what must occur. Original sin was conceived as a moral and personal debt owed to God, which needed to be repaid. Humanity was fallen, so we could not make the sacrifice and so pay the debt, because no matter how well intentioned and fully undertaken our offering might be, it would always remain imperfect. In Christian theology, it is the perfect Son who becomes the perfect man and can make the perfect sacrifice to the perfect God, and so the breach is healed, and heaven is again wedded to earth. It is from this theology that the Protestant satisfaction theology was born, that God's wrath or anger was finally and totally "satisfied." Catholic theology developed a theory of atonement describing the death of Jesus, as in the pattern of the atoning sacrifices of the temple, as definitively reconciling creation to God.

There are many questions that arise from this theology. In Genesis, God creates humanity with the freedom to choose, and then seems angry when they exercise that choice. As represented by the serpent, evil is created by God—a very problematic proposition for a truly and fully loving being—who seems to invest the serpent with stronger powers of persuasion than he has. Having been set up for a fall, Adam and Eve are punished for their sin by being alienated from God, as expressed in them roaming the earth. Subsequent presentations of God's anger at our lack of fidelity can seem to suggest that God is no better than we are, brooding and angry, since humanity was created for a situation that we did not create and that was the result of a bad choice when it was offered. Furthermore, it can be argued that God appears imperfect until the final repenting sacrifice is made, and somehow we had to do something, in Jesus and to Jesus in the crucifixion, to fulfill this need in God.

Christian teaching that Jesus' death pays off the debt of our sin to God begins with St. Paul's Letter to the Romans: "God put [him] forward as a sacrifice of atonement by his blood, effective through faith" (3:25). And later, he explicitly draws out the parallel with Adam in an understandably literal reading of Genesis: "Therefore, just as sin came into the world through one man [Adam], and death came through sin, and so death spread to all because all have sinned...for just as by the one man's disobedience the many were made sinners, so by the one man's obedience the many will be made righteous" (5:12, 19). St. Paul argues this was the work of our redemption.

Understanding this concept of redemption holds the key to another way forward. As noted in *Where the Hell Is God?*, the word *redemption* literally means "buying back." It comes from the practice in the ancient world where there were two types of slaves— ones who were born or forced into slavery, usually for life, and others who paid off a debt or a crime by becoming a slave, usually for a period of time. The second type of slaves could be set free when someone else paid their debts, or the ransom their master now demanded for them was settled. They would, then, either be the slave of the purchaser or set free completely.

St. Paul introduced this metaphor into Christian theology to describe how we, who are enslaved by our destructive behavior, gained a liberator in Christ, who entered into a sinful world and subjected himself to its violence and death in order to set us free. At its best, the notion of Christ the Redeemer shows us that we do not have to live destructively anymore. Now claimed by the love of Christ, we are no longer slaves, but his friends; indeed, through the redeeming work of Christ, we have been welcomed into God's family and shown the path to life.

For Christians the paschal mystery—the life, death, and resurrection of Jesus—is the central paradigm around which our faith in God is constructed. However, the Word of God did not become one with us as a human being simply and only to die. If that were baldly true, then why did God spare him from the outcome of the most unjust theological story in the New Testament— Matthew's slaughter of the innocents (2:13–23)? If Jesus had been murdered by Herod at two years of age, then God could have got his blood sacrifice over nice and early. If all God wanted was the perfect blood offering of his only Son for the sake of appeasing his anger, why did Jesus not leave Nazareth, stir up plenty of trouble around Galilee (as he did), and then march straight into Jerusalem and offend everyone and get crucified early on? It would not have been hard. If Jesus had simply been sent "to die," then what was the reason for his hidden years and his years of public ministry? They were not for God's sake, but for ours.

Jesus did not simply and only come to die. Rather, Jesus came to live, and as a result of the courageous and radical way he lived his life, and the saving love he embodied for all humanity, he threatened the political, social, and religious authorities of his day so much that they executed him. This is an easier way for us to make sense of the predictions of the passion. Jesus was not clairvoyant; he was a full and true human being and therefore had informed but limited knowledge. His full and true divinity cannot obliterate his humanity or he would be playacting at being human. His divinity is seen in and through the uncompromisingly loving, just, and sacrificial way he lived within the bounds of his humanity.

Many of the most morally courageous people in history knew that their personal life and liberty were threatened because of what they were saying or how they were living. They may not have known beforehand they would be executed or murdered or assassinated, but they could read the signs of their times well enough to predict that there were serious consequences to the freedom they were embodying and to which they were attracting other people. Sometimes they spoke or wrote about the cost of the stands they took. In this regard they reflect Jesus Christ. Our martyrs are not Christian versions of suicide bombers. They do not go looking for death in any active sense. That would be the ultimate betrayal of God's gift of life. However, they know that they may die as a result of witnessing to their faith and the demand for justice that must flow from it. In their lives and deaths they follow the pattern of Jesus. He did not seek death for its own sake, but he would not and could not live any other way than faithfully, hopefully, and lovingly. In his day, as in our own, this is immensely threatening to those whose power base is built on values opposed to these virtues. The world continues to silence and sideline people who live out the Christian virtues and values now, just as Jesus was thought to be ultimately sidelined in his crucifixion. But God had the last word on the death of Jesus: life.

For most of Christian history the question that has vexed many believers seems to be, "Why did Jesus die?" I think the better question might be, "Why was Jesus killed?" This question puts the last days of Jesus' suffering and death in an entirely new perspective.

With this new perspective, we can stand before the cross and listen to Jesus in John's Gospel say, "I have come that you may have life, and have it to the full." This life is not about the perfect Son of the perfect Father making the perfect sacrifice to get us back in God's good books, and thereby saving us. Our God does not deal in death, but life. Everything in the New Testament demonstrates this, even the grand apocalyptic narratives about the end of time, which show all the hallmarks of an inspired rabbinic teacher drawing big strokes on the largest of canvases. Jesus did not intend us to take this imagery literally. I assume the experience of judgment will not actually be a livestock muster of sheep and goats. The lesson behind the imagery, however, is a real one for us to learn. God's compassion and love will ultimately see that justice is done. He will hear the cry of the poor and we will be called to account in the next life for what we have done and what we have failed to do in this life.

On Good Friday, we find God in Jesus Christ confronting evil, death, and destruction head-on, and staring it down, so that light and life have the last word.

BECAUSE OF JESUS' LIFE, DEATH, AND RESURRECTION, CHRISTIANS BELIEVE THAT ETERNAL LIFE IS OPENED TO HUMANITY. THEREFORE, HOW CAN ANYONE BELIEVE IN A LOVING GOD WHO CAN ALSO DAMN PEOPLE TO HELL? HASN'T THIS THEOLOGY JUST BEEN ABOUT RELIGIONS MAINTAINING THEIR SOCIAL CONTROL OVER ADHERENTS?

Given what I have said about Jesus not coming among us primarily and only to die *for* our sins, but moreover died at the hands *of* our sinfulness, then his life, death, and resurrection show us how to *live*—even through our suffering and death to life eternal. There is no question that the way in which God's judgment and condemnation has been presented by some Christians over the millennia was a form of social control, but those days are now gone. If there are some Catholics preaching hellfire and damnation as the reason for faith these days, then they must be disappointed that very few people are listening to them and worried about it. The rates of religious practice, which was often the way a believer tried to keep an angry God on his or her side and thereby avoid hell, have plummeted in almost every Western country. However, as we noted in the previous chapter, one of the major shifts in theology over the last fifty years has been from being driven by fear to being drawn by love. I am not a Christian, a Catholic, a Jesuit, or a priest because I am trying to "save my soul" from hell. I do what I do because it is my response to a loving God's invitation to faith, hope, and love.

Even when heaven, hell, and purgatory were presented graphically, there were always problems with the literalness of the images. Classical theology has always held that in eternal life there will not be time and space, mind and body. Heaven is about transcending the bounds of earth. So even when preachers talked about "fire and brimstone" and "physical pangs," it was a poetic way to describe the indescribable, because we cannot undergo physical torments if we don't have a physical body.

Our Catholic theology about heaven, hell, and purgatory enshrines a profound religious truth—that our life here on earth impacts on our eternal life.

I have confident faith that God would not deny heaven to the many people we know who faithfully, lovingly, and hopefully lived their lives as best as they could. The Scriptures give us confidence to know that God does not concern himself with small matters. But what about the individuals and societies whose behavior destroys other people? What about those who never repent of the sexual abuse of a child, their physical and emotional violence, being a serial adulterer, and murderer? What about those who refuse to share from their excess with those who have nothing in our world? And what about those who don't care or don't want to know about the fallout from their apathy or the consequences involved in the luxury of ignorance? None of these people, none of us, is ever too far from the compassion and forgiveness of God, but I am also convinced that God takes our free decisions on serious matters very seriously.

Before offering some reflections on heaven, hell, and purgatory, let us consider the "soul." If eternal life transcends time and space, mind and body, then we cannot "do time" in purgatory in the traditional sense, and we need to clarify what survives us when we die. Christians have always said that while our body dies, our spirit or soul is what survives and endures.

In an increasingly secular society, it is striking how the word *soul* persists in ordinary conversation. Many nonreligious people use this most religious of terms to describe another person. We often hear how others are lonely, distressed, or lost souls. It can be said that someone has a "beautiful soul" or that a piece of music, a painting, or other works of art "stirred my soul." We describe mellow jazz as "soulful" and still alert others to distress by an SOS, "save our souls." These uses of the word reinforce St. Thomas Aquinas's teaching that the soul makes us human, and set us apart from other animals. Nearly all the great religions of the world believe in a soul or its equivalent—something that survives the annihilation of the body in death.

It is my view that whatever else might characterize the soul, memory is an integral part of it. Why?

I have done several funerals of people who have suffered from Alzheimer's disease. These are rarely very sad occasions because the family invariably says that they "lost" their loved one months or years ago. Why? Because increasingly their loved one couldn't remember anyone or anything. We hold to caring for the body from the womb to the tomb because we believe that human dignity must always be respected. There are now theories about how even the memories of the circumstances of our conception and birth have a bearing on the way we live our lives. It is also apparent that even when people seem to have lost their memory or are unconscious, that there is some recognition of some things at a very deep level.

Soul as memory means that when I meet God face to face, I will remember who I am and how I lived, and God will remember me. It's also a comfort for us to think that we will be reunited with those we have loved who have died before us, because we remember each other.

This is not the last word on the matter, since it raises the question of the humanity of those who we do not think can remember anything. Are they any less human? I would say that every human being has inalienable rights because they may have memory at their deepest level, and because we know in faith that each and every one is known and remembered by God from conception to death.

So what happens after our soul leaves our body, "commended to the mercy of God," as we used to say? Well, *the* great parable of God's mercy is the best place to start.

In the story of the Prodigal Son, we have the worst kid in town making a return and being received by his foolishly loving father.

Rather than think of heaven, hell, and purgatory as places where we do time, imagine if they are experiences or states. I wonder if a goodly number of souls, people who have done their best on earth, according to their lights, make the journey home. The Father rushes out to greet them. They start their speech, but the loving Father cuts them off, and welcomes them home. That has to be the experience of heaven—welcomed to the eternal banquet!

However, some make the journey home and start the speech, which the loving Father allows them to finish—such has been the enormity of their deliberately chosen, free, and seriously destructive behavior toward others and themselves in this world. At the end of the speech they are forgiven, now fully aware of the gravity of their sinfulness, and its impact. And it costs us to say, "I'm sorry," and it costs the Father to forgive (like a husband or wife who genuinely forgives the other for adultery). That might be purgatory—an experience in cleansing, of being purgated, not in anger or suffering, but in love—painful love as it might be.

And for a very few who have deliberately and knowingly rejected God throughout their whole lives—God in all his forms: in faith, hope, and love—they make the journey to the Father and come face to face with pure love. They do not start the speech, they are not welcomed in, because God respects their freedom so much that he allows them to do what they have done all their lives—see love and walk away. That has to be hell—to know love, to have glimpsed it, and still turn around and walk away because they always have. The ultimate absence: a remembering soul that saw love and chose otherwise.

HOW CAN WOMEN BELIEVE IN A GOD WHOSE FOLLOWERS WON'T HAVE WOMEN AS LEADERS?

In speaking with young Catholic women, it is rare that this issue does not emerge strongly for many of them as a problem in their life of faith. They see that in nearly every other sphere of life, women are, at least theoretically and now enshrined by law in most countries, able to hold any office of principal authority in any institution other than religious ones. Certainly, some women and men have walked away from a faith in a so-called male God, and some from the Catholic Church, in particular, because they see it as inherently discriminatory. Though the issues are larger than ordination, the discussion often centers on the Church stating that it cannot ordain women to the priesthood.

Though the status of women is vastly different throughout the world, and sometimes very tragic in some cultures, even within these differing social expectations, Pope John Paul II said that women's rights to dignity and human flourishing are given by God and should always be defended by the Church.[13] This is even more true in nations where women's basic human rights are criminally and tragically abused. Given the differing social expectations and even though the issues are larger than ordination, current debates, both inside and outside the church, often center on the Church stating that it cannot, has no authority to, ordain women to the priesthood.

The following is a brief summary, which hardly conveys all the arguments presented in the libraries of books written on both sides of this debate. There are six main reasons the Church says it has no power to ordain women: first, Jesus did not ordain any women—that the first apostles were all male; second, the all-male priesthood has been an unbroken tradition in the Church's history; third, because in sacramental liturgies the priest acts in the name and person of Jesus—having a male priest establishes a clearer iconography or identification between the priest and Jesus; fourth, while women and men are created equal by God, they have differing gender-specific roles, and to confuse these is to harm the balance of our human condition; fifth, the priesthood should not be seen as an office of power to be obtained and used, but as an order of self-sacrificing service; finally, the Church has been a place where women are not oppressed but where their many and manifest gifts have flourished and been celebrated from Mary, the Mother of God, who is first among (all) the saints; to St. Mary Magdalene, who was the "Apostle to the Apostles"; to an array of mystics, saints, founders, martyrs, and scholars.

The critics of these arguments claim, first, that Jesus may have had twelve male apostles, but he had and commissioned many female disciples, some of whom were his most faithful followers. They also challenge that he "ordained" anyone in the way we now use that term and understand that office. Set against the customs of his day, his attitudes and practices toward women and their leadership was radical. Second, the argument of an unbroken tradition of an "all-male" priesthood is not as watertight as some claim. There seems to be some evidence of women presiding over house churches, Mary Magdalene and Junia are called apostles, and women were deacons for several centuries; third, at sacramental liturgies, the priest acts in the name and person of the Risen Christ in whom "there is no longer Jew or Greek, there is no longer slave or free, there is no longer male and female; for all of you are one in Christ Jesus" (Gal 3:28). While the Church has let go of Jesus' culture and religion as prerequisites for Christian ordination, gender, apparently, remains the only nonnegotiable factor. Fourth, given that we no longer read the Book of Genesis literally, the gender roles that emerge there should not be absolutized, but should rather be interpreted as a theological construction around social determinations; fifth, there is nothing wrong in talking about access to governance when it combines the right and just use of power as well as modeling self-sacrificing service. Finally, for all the Church's rhetoric about the great gifts of women, and especially about motherhood, there has not been a corresponding and meaningful harnessing of their gifts for leadership at every level of the Church's life.

While the judgment of a male cleric might be seen to be overly defensive of the Church's position, there is an important distinction to be made in this debate between ordination and leadership. In the final chapter of this book I will be exploring the lives of thirteen Christians who inspire my faith in God and belonging to the Church. Among this group are Catherine McAuley and Mary MacKillop, who, along with Mary Ward, Nano Nagle, and Mary Aitkenhead, just to name a few, had to put up with appalling discrimination from male church officials of their day. The only historical comfort we can draw from what they suffered is that their detractors are now forgotten to history, but each of them is now or is in the process of being declared a saint, and rightly so.

While ordination gives a priest sacramental and structural power, it does not necessarily bestow upon him the gift of leadership, which is endorsed by a leader's followers. There are some priests who may be ordained, but they lead no one anywhere. There are women who have never and will never be ordained, but their leadership is inspiring. If we look beyond sacramental leadership—and I concede that is a central reality of the Catholic Church's life—and examine education, healthcare, welfare, pastoral care, and spirituality, we find that in almost every Western country in the world, women's leadership is indispensable. In fact, if they stopped leading and working in all these ministries, the entire mission and daily ministry of the church would come to a halt. It might be a good thing if the women of the church went on strike one week in order to remind the men who it is that are actually running this "show" in and through their sometimes heroic, self-sacrificing service.

Similarly, it is important that we recognize the equal dignity of women and men created in the image and likeness of God, and their complementarity and mutuality, so that it translates into the active participation of women throughout all levels of decision making in the Church, a reexamination of the nature of non-priestly ministry with the exploration of more inclusive roles for men and women, and a reform of practices that do not promote the equality of men and women.

Pope Francis seems keen to initiate such a discussion on the role of women in the life of the Church:

> Women must have a greater presence in the decision-making areas of the church....[They] cannot be limited to the fact of being an altar server or the president of Caritas, the catechist....No!...We need to create still broader opportunities for a more inclusive female presence in the Church....Demands that the legitimate rights of women be respected, based on the firm conviction that men and women are equal in dignity, present the Church with profound and challenging questions which cannot be lightly evaded.[14]

Whether he would go as far as Cardinal Martini[15] and Bishop Wcela in calling for women to be ordained deacons is yet to be seen.

> Ordaining women as deacons who have the necessary personal, spiritual, intellectual and pastoral qualities would give their indispensable role in the life of the

church a new degree of official recognition, both in their ministry and in their direct connection to their diocesan bishop for assignments and faculties. In addition to providing such women with the grace of the sacrament, ordination would enable them to exercise diaconal service in the teaching, sanctifying, and governing functions of the church; it would also make it possible for them to hold ecclesiastical offices now limited to those in sacred orders.[16]

Future discussion about women becoming cardinals is both theologically and theoretically possible.[17] Regardless of this discussion, it is incontestable that women should participate more and more at every level of decision making: locally, nationally, and internationally. Rather than walk away from the Church, young women will hopefully stay, name, and shame any discrimination they experience in God's name, enabling all of us to create a more inclusive and empowering Church for them and their daughters and sons.

GIVEN THAT JESUS WAS A SIMPLE MAN WHO ADVOCATED FOR THE POOR, ISN'T THE CHURCH'S WEALTH AND POWER A MAJOR STUMBLING BLOCK TO BELIEF?

Every major study of belief and unbelief says that for many people it is not only a deity that is the major stumbling block to religious faith, but also the lives of religious individuals and collectives who claim to follow that God. It is chastening indeed to think that the church, universally and locally, can be the greatest obstacle to anyone believing in the God we proclaim. It is a good challenge for us to practice what we preach and to follow Jesus' service, humility, and simplicity. It seems that Pope Francis's example has gone some way in this regard.

It is true that Jesus was a poor man who preached a gospel about lifting up the poor, the marginalized and the oppressed, and who said that not only do we have an obligation to share but that we will be happiest when we are free of the possessions that keep us from loving God and our neighbor. He also knew that love of money was one of the greatest dangers to us losing our very selves. There is no question that for the first three hundred years of the Christian church's life, it lived the simplicity Jesus lived. In fact, given that many people died for their Christian faith, their witness to a sacrificial life is above reproach.

The defining change, for good and for ill, comes after Constantine's vision in AD 312 that lead him to convert to Christianity and use his new faith as a unifying force in his empire. By AD 380, Christianity had become the state religion. On the positive side, this meant that Christians were no longer martyred for their faith. On the downside, the Christian church now received imperial patronage, had confiscated property returned to it and gained, and sometimes abused, civil prestige and power. We can easily see why, after generations of martyrs and persecutions, Christians saw this development as a sign of God's blessing. With the demise of the Western Roman Empire in 476, when Romulus Augustus was deposed, the Church began to fill the temporal and spiritual vacuum in the West, and became a threat to the power of the emperor of the Eastern Empire.

In fairness, the Christian church is the only single institution in Western society to have survived so long. Today, therefore, it is easy to judge what later became the Roman Catholic Church and its subsequent claim on power and wealth as a betrayal of what Jesus proclaimed. It certainly was a betrayal, but it also provided social stability and cohesion in very desolate times. For over a thousand years, there was a varied but often mutually dysfunctional relationship between temporal powers and the popes of the Roman church, in which it took on all the trappings of the earthly kingdom Jesus rejected. Innocent III (1198–1216) and Boniface VIII (1294–1303) embody the culmination of papal power over church, state, appointments, land, armies, and wealth.

So much for history, except that without noting this development, it is impossible to understand where we are now. We have no idea how wealthy the Catholic Church actually is. Against the monolithic institution that many assume the Church to be, it is, in fact, a communion of churches, albeit one where the pope "has full, supreme and universal power" (Vatican Council II, *Lumen Gentium* 22). Nevertheless, what makes me Catholic is not any personal affection for a particular pope, but the more ancient tradition of being in communion (literally, we can receive the same Holy Communion) with my local bishop, who is, in turn, in communion with the bishop of Rome. At the time of writing, there were 2,946 dioceses in the Catholic world, and though they have to annually report to Rome on their local church, many would not know the actual wealth of all the local holdings. Suffice it to say, some dioceses are very wealthy and some are desperately poor. Being private, not-for-profit institutions, almost none of these dioceses have to give full financial disclosure to civil authorities. No doubt, this will change in the years to come.

In 2012, the *Economist* estimated that the U.S. Catholic Church was worth around $170 billion, of which $150 billion was estimated to be in the assets and real estate of U.S. Catholic healthcare, welfare, and education institutions. Trying to put a value on the Vatican City State is nearly impossible. The best estimate is around $10 to $15 billion. It has 15 percent of the value of the listed shares on the Italian stock market, which is thought to be valued at $1.2 billion. The annual running budget of the Vatican is approximately $325 million, with $115 million of that coming from the 5 million tourists who enter one or more of the museums each year. The shortfall is made up from investments and donations from dioceses around the world. It employs 2,800 employees. It is a vast enterprise and a long way from the simplicity and poverty of the first community around Jesus.

In his book *Things You Get for Free*, Michael McGirr tells the story of going on pilgrimage to Rome with his mother. Maureen McGirr had always wanted to see St. Peter's Basilica. Michael records the big day.

Once you get inside, however, St. Peter's strips you bare.

Mum took a few steps forward into the cavernous gloom and stopped. I looked up into the dome that Michelangelo designed late in life: he never lived to see it finished. In that moment, hundreds of visitors rushed past.

"What on earth are they trying to prove?" I wasn't sure if Mum was talking about the building or all the people rushing past. Officials were still clearing away the cheap plastic stacking chairs which come out for big masses. They were not part of the original design. I was distracted by the noise.

"When you think," said Mum, leaving her sentence unfinished....

"When you think what?" I asked....

"I don't know. When you think."

"What?" I was getting testy with her.

Mum drew in breath to say something important.

"When you think that Jesus had nothing."

It was a naked response. For seventy years, this building had stood as the physical centre of Mum's religion. This was her pilgrimage to Mecca. Yet her response was almost revulsion. I want to put a brake on her reaction and jolly her along and tell her that Jesus would rather have had this as a monument than the Empire State Building or the Crown Casino.[18]

No matter how much we try to ignore it, or play it down, the call to simplicity of lifestyle, detachment, and sharing what we have are essential elements in the teaching of Jesus, the way he lived his own life, and they still challenge us today.

On the other side of the ledger, it is good to remember that the wealth of the Church is not only and simply about power for its own sake. For a start, the Vatican would need to financially assist hundreds of its 2,946 dioceses to provide local services, on every level, for believer and unbeliever alike. In many countries, the Church, albeit sometimes with the support of tax-free concessions granted to other charities too, is, outside government, the single largest provider of healthcare, welfare, and education in that nation. The money raised every year by Caritas, which is itself a confederation of 164 Roman Catholic relief agencies in two hundred countries, as well as Catholic Mission, Catholic Relief Services in the USA, the Catholic Agency for Overseas Development in the UK, the Pontifical Mission Societies operating in 120 countries, the Missionary Childhood Association, Jesuit Refugee Service, Mercy Refugee Service, and the St. Vincent de Paul Society, just to name a few of the hundreds and hundreds of relief and service organizations sponsored or promoted by the Catholic Church, serve many millions of people a year, regardless of their religious, social, or economic backgrounds.

Even though there is a valid argument that the Vatican museums could sell the art and give the money to the poor (though it would be hard to get Michelangelo off the roof and walls of the Sistine Chapel), I am not sure it is the only valid argument. Last year the Vatican Museum was the fifth most visited gallery in the world, and those of us who have been there know most people visit simply to see the Sistine Chapel. However, even if the holdings were sold, they would almost certainly go into the hands of private buyers, thirty-nine of the top fifty of whom last year were from China. Most of the top fifty buyers do not donate or show their works in public galleries. As complex as the commissioning and acquisition of our Catholic artistic heritage may be, at least now it can be enjoyed by generation after generation of ordinary people. The sale of it now would be good for temporary public relations for the Vatican, but it would have minimal impact on the life of the poor.

So while extraordinary events in history, along with criminal abuse of power and mutual alliances, have left us with the legacy of the real estate and art and architecture we own, selling it all in our following of Jesus in poverty is one option. Deciding to use all the resources at our disposal, not only to feed the poor but to change the international structures that keep them that way, is another option. The real stumbling block is learning from the avarice and triumphalism of some of the previous generations of the Church. Living simply with what we need rather than what we want, sharing everything with the poor, who are at the center of the Gospel, and being a voice for the voiceless in many circles in which the Church lives might be the even bigger and more exciting challenges.

WHY FOLLOW ANY RELIGION'S MORAL CODE? WHY NOT SIMPLY FOLLOW YOUR OWN MORAL CODE?

The short answer is that there is nothing stopping anyone living "according to his or her lights," as St. Ignatius Loyola would say. In fact, the Catholic Church says that because everyone will have to account for who they are, what they choose, and what they do and what they fail to do, then every person must live according to the dictates of his or her informed conscience. Even if the Church thinks that a particular conscience is in error, and the choices that flow from it are poor ones, they are obliged to follow their conscience, knowing that they will be held to account for their decisions. The reality is, however, that without some sense of a personal relationship with Jesus, Christian morality can be reduced to the rule book of a stern judge.

While we have made Christianity very complex indeed, it is quite simple: love God, love your neighbor, and love yourself. Jesus said that on these things hang all the Law and Prophets. Jesus took that Mosaic Law, which tended to be about what we should not do, and expressed his approach to morality in three positive laws of love.

Not that the Ten Commandments don't have anything to offer anymore. They do, but there are not just ten of them. First, the Decalogue is already a summary of the 613 commandments in the Mosaic Law, and most of these Christians have rightly and easily left behind. Second, the language therein does not work anymore. The idea of "coveting" anything, but especially "wives, slaves, ox and ass" highlights the need for a creative makeover. When that happens, one discovers that they still have something to say to us, and through this process we discover something important about religious thought. Often what it enshrines is a hard-won lesson from human experience. Some of it is bound to a time and place, like almost all the dietary laws, but other teachings, when properly understood and updated, contain great wisdom.

In "Preaching to the Modern Pagans," controversial journalist Bryan Appleyard tells how he interviewed a person who kept quoting the Ten Commandments at length. Later, he decided to read them for the first time since childhood and was struck by their insightfulness into the human character. Appleyard thought all the Ten Commandments needed was a makeover so that we can reclaim their power.

We are used to hearing the first Commandment say, "I am the LORD your God, who brought you out of the land of Egypt, out of the house of slavery; you shall have no other gods before me." Appleyard says this basically means *be serious*. "You shall not make for yourself an idol, whether in the form of anything that is in heaven above, or that is on the earth beneath, or that is in the water under the earth." *Get real*. "You shall not make wrongful use of the name of the LORD your God, for the LORD will not acquit anyone who misuses his name." *Be humble, we are creatures, not the Creator*. "Remember the sabbath day, and keep it holy." *Be quiet*. "Honor your father and your mother, so that your days may be long in the land that the LORD your God is giving you." *Respect age*. "You shall not murder." *Do not kill, for all murder is suicide*. "You shall not commit adultery." *Mean what you say*. "You shall not steal." *Do not steal, or all the world will die.* "You shall not bear false witness against your neighbor." *Honor others, their frailties are usually your own*. "You shall not covet your neighbor's house; you shall not covet your neighbor's wife, or male or female slave, or ox, or donkey, or anything that belongs to your neighbor." *Be kind, be generous, and don't screw around.*

Even many of those who don't like religion could easily say

yes to Appleyard's makeover of the Ten Commandments. Believers and unbelievers, however, are never going to agree on Jesus' makeover of them in his three laws of love, because we cannot agree on the love of God as the ground for all love that follows.

Christian morality is helpful because it is, at its best, two thousand years of us reflecting on complex human beings making complex human choices. In the New Testament, St. Paul tells us that the greatest moral virtues are faith, hope, and love. Later, in book II of the *Summa Theologica*, St. Thomas Aquinas (1225–74) reflected on Aristotle's (384–322 BC) ethics and went on to outline out how faith, hope, and charity are practically applied through the naturally acquired virtues, which Aquinas came to call the cardinal virtues: justice, temperance, fortitude, and prudence. These were ways in which Christians interacted with a complex world, discerned where virtues reside, developed the excellence of their character, the process by which they thought through situations clearly, and made careful choices. Aquinas maintained that believers and nonbelievers shared in the divinely infused virtues, but all could attain the other cardinal virtues. He argued that everyone is able to perfect the virtues, but it is the believer who has the ability to call on God's love to perfect everything.

This is expressed here far too simply to be fair to Aquinas, but for brevity, God can be found wherever faith, hope, love, justice, temperance, fortitude, and prudence are in evidence. Not that Aquinas was only interested in the balance and beauty in the world. In the fourth century, Evagrius Ponticus was the first to list eight evil desires, which were later developed by Pope Gregory the Great and later refined and branded by Aquinas as the seven deadly sins: pride, greed, envy, anger, lust, gluttony, and sloth. For Aquinas, these sins were not just the worst sins we could commit, they were where humanity gets entrapped.

First, for Christians, the problem is that the wider world now presents and promotes the seven deadly sins as glamorous and normal. By glamorous I mean that we are sometimes told that being proud, greedy, envious, angry, lustful, gluttonous, and slothful is not deadly at all—it's life giving, and can lead to happiness, popularity, and success. As a Christian, this is not true. In fact, I find working against the deadly sins in my life liberating. The second thing that is sometimes promoted is that destructive behavior is normal, that is, there is nothing we can do about it because it is the reality of the human condition. Christianity does not regard pride, greed, envy, anger, lust, gluttony, and sloth as the normal destiny of a human being. We are better than our worst behavior, and we can pick ourselves up when we fall, make amends or new choices, and start again.

Christian morality is trying to be the most loving person possible by living out the virtues in our daily lives. We are not world rejecters, we are world affirmers, and every Christian is called to participate in his or her culture as critic, shaper, receiver, and translator. In living out our morality, we recognize that with every gift in our life comes the responsibility to use that gift well not just for our personal benefit but for the wider common good too. Furthermore, while we want to affirm all the ways our morality complements other religious moral codes, and those of individuals, there are some moral choices that we can never affirm. The dignity of human life from the womb to the tomb is one critical example. Because we believe there are consequences to what we choose that have implications for all of humanity, we do not think morality is only personal. It is always a social act too. When I choose something poor, then I am diminished, and therefore the world is a slightly more diminished place too. While there are personal moral choices, there are never private ones. I am the lump sum of my decisions. We advocate for what we believe is the best way for humanity to flourish. Because we believe God has given the human family a common human condition, then we also believe in a common human morality. When we promote what we think is for the common good, others sometimes accuse us of being judgmental.

One of the more unfortunate things that has happened in recent years is a belief that we should no longer judge one another's behavior. We hear expressions like, "We are in no position to judge," "You can't judge them," or "They can't judge us." On this point we are quite confused. For Christians, one of the seven gifts of the Holy Spirit is right judgment. I assume that when we say, "Don't judge," what we are trying to say is "don't condemn." However, there is a world of difference between these two ideas. There is not a page in the Gospels when Jesus did not judge the people around him. However, we are explicitly told in John 8, and in many other places besides, that Jesus never condemned anyone. Condemnation belongs to God alone, but by being an ethical Christian, we need to cultivate the gift of compassionate judgment and critical consumption and try not to be seduced by attitudes, responses, and appetites that are not life giving and life sustaining.

IF CHRISTIANS HAVE TO BELIEVE IN THEIR FAIRY TALES, CAN THEY JUST DO SO PRIVATELY AND STAY OUT OF POLITICS AND LAW?

Let's begin with the middle part of the question: fairy tales. These days we hear this one frequently—that all religious people believe in fairy tales. I have already said that I am an atheist toward all other religions but Christianity. As a member of a religion who has dismissed and denounced every other position than my own for generations, sometimes with tragic consequences and legitimating murderous behavior to keep others silent, I can only advise against such cynicism. Although there are many definitions of what constitutes a fairy tale, common elements include a purposely made-up folkloric story, almost always involving magic, illuminating an ethical choice, and regularly warning about the moral consequences of a poor decision. There are a few passages in the Bible that might fit that definition. I have already outlined the vast array of literary genres we find in that library of books, but to sum up and dismiss someone's religious beliefs as simply and only a belief in fairy tales is intolerant. Sadly, we still find in some religious groups people who condemn those who do not share their particular beliefs. Either side of the belief fence, these cynical dismissals are as inaccurate as they are disrespectful.

The majority of Christians I know never deride or condemn people whose experiences lead them to very different conclusions about where we come from, why we are here, and where we are going. At least, they would be respectful of another's sincerely held position, and often want to know where it comes from, why they hold it, and what implications flow from it. That is my position in regard to other schools of religious thought as well as secular humanists and atheists.

Nearly every ethical system in the world, religious or secular, outlines fundamental principles of our shared humanity, our interdependence on one another, and respect for the natural order as a way for us to live peacefully together and to avoid suffering—a perfectly good place for dialogue to begin.

The second part of the question is not as nuanced as it could be. In the previous chapter, we noted that, while some atheists and secular humanists seem to be obsessed with religion, others could not care less about it until religion has an impact on an issue of public policy with which they disagree. There are thirty-four Organisation for Economic Co-operation and Development (OECD) countries in the world: Australia, Austria, Belgium, Canada, Chile, Czech Republic, Denmark, Estonia, Finland, France, Germany, Greece, Hungary, Iceland, Ireland, Israel, Italy, Japan, Korea, Luxembourg, Mexico, the Netherlands, New Zealand, Norway, Poland, Portugal, the Slovak Republic, Slovenia, Spain, Sweden, Switzerland, Turkey, the United Kingdom, and the United States of America; all, except four, have long and complex associations with Christianity. Given that we only have a few atheistic nations with which to compare and contrast, it can be asserted that Christianity has formed them for the better more than the worse. Furthermore, other religions are significant in the other four countries: Judaism is the predominant religion of Israel; 99 percent of Turkey is Muslim; 93 percent of the population in Japan identify themselves as either Shinto or Buddhist; and in South Korea, over 58 percent are either Buddhist or Christian, while 52 percent of all Koreans state they have no religion. Interestingly, even in countries where there is a large number who say they hold no religion, some of these nations have a state church: Greece, Denmark, Iceland, Norway, and the United Kingdom. Other OECD countries have special constitutional arrangements for one Christian denomination: Poland, Spain, Finland, Sweden, and twenty-four of the twenty-six cantons in Switzerland. Germany, Austria, and Italy have no formal recognition of any religion in their constitutions; but the state does collect a controversial church tax to support religious activities, as does Denmark, Sweden, Finland, Iceland, and all the twenty-six cantons in Switzerland.

The argument on the right role of religion in public policy, therefore, is more complex than it first appears. If Abraham Lincoln is right in saying that "democracy is the government of the people, by the people, for the people," then public policy must reflect the majority view. At the time of writing, France, the Czech Republic, Germany, and South Korea are the four OECD countries where atheists are approaching 30 percent or more of their respective populations. As noted in the previous chapter, the number of citizens who state that they have no belief is growing significantly in all countries. However, for now the majority of all OECD countries profess to have some form of religious belief. Therefore, in a democracy, religious believers are fully entitled to participate in the process of political debate and have a hand in shaping the laws that flow from it. It is also true that some religious adherents may disagree with their church's position on one or several issues of the common good. The legalization of illicit drugs, pornography, avoidance of taxation, software piracy, euthanasia, environmental issues, abortion, just distribution of wealth, contraception, rights of workers, adultery, IVF, homosexuality, and immigration issues are just some of the debates I have had with practicing Catholics who have differing views from the official teaching of the Catholic Church.

Two extremes are to be avoided: first, a theocracy, where religious law is the only law of the land. There are only three theocracies left in the world: the Holy See, Iran, and Tibet. Sharia law, however, is followed in Afghanistan, Iran, Mauritania, Saudi

Arabia, Somalia, Sudan, Yemen, and some Islamic states within Nigeria. Second, it is equally disturbing for a pluralistic democracy to stifle debate among its citizens. This is not to say that religions should not be accorded any special privilege in political debate. Our advocacy for any social policy should rise or fall on the basis of the arguments and its contribution for the common good, regardless of its religious motivations. Religions in Western democracies are now in the game of winning hearts and minds on the basis of their ability to intelligently and truthfully persuade, counsel, and warn their fellow citizens in regard to a particular choice and its potential consequences. The same status should be afforded to all other parties in the debate as well, and then the decisions left to what we hope would be a well-informed legislature.

However, if the wide resentment of those with no religion grows to such a point that all Christian aspects of most OECD countries were dismantled, then it could have far-reaching and maybe unforeseen implications. St. Valentine's Day, named for a third-century Roman martyr who died out of love for Christ, would have to be renamed Cupid's day, except Cupid was the Greek god of love. The feasts of Christmas, Good Friday, and Easter, and the public holidays surrounding them, would need to be dropped or transferred or rebranded as secular public commemorations. All references to the Christmas season—the exchange of Christmas gifts, trees, carols, cribs, and dinners—would have to be publicly abandoned. Any child care center that receives any public funding would need to jettison the Christmas nativity play. Professor Dawkins might be sad to see some of that go: "Nor do I shy away from singing the familiar and much loved Christmas songs that I sang for years in choir or at home. 'Silent Night' still can bring a tear to my eye because it recalls memories of childhood."[19] Even Santa Claus would have to be reinvented, based as he is on the fourth-century St. Nicholas, Bishop of Myra, who started giving gifts to the poor in his parish on Christmas Eve around AD 365.

All references to God on secular coats of arms, money, and in all oaths of allegiance, and vows to tell the truth, "so help me

God," will have to be dismissed. There could be no swearing on a Bible, ever, and no religious prayers uttered anywhere in the civic arena. National songs and hymns would need a makeover so that God would no longer be saving the queen, defending New Zealand, or making Canada glorious and free. Presumably, this would be the end of the taxpayer funded British royal coronations, funerals, and weddings in the Church of England, a very popular public broadcast around the world, because they would now have to be private religious events.

All references directly related to the cross of Christ would have to be changed: the Red Cross, the Victoria Cross, the Distinguished Service Cross, and the Cross of Valor do not owe their origins to any old cross but to the one upon which Jesus died. Even Hollywood would need to be renamed because in 1886 it was called that by the devout Methodist, Mrs. H. H. Wilcox, after the cross of Christ.[20] We would need new secular symbols as we dropped the stars of David, Christian crosses, and crescents on civic flags and banners.

No doubt, choirs and orchestras that receive any share of government funding or assistance would not be allowed to perform any type of religious music. Most of Bach would be banned. All religious art, including indigenous religious art and artifacts, would have to be withdrawn from public view or sold to private collectors. Furthermore, public libraries could raise money for the poor by selling off all their religious volumes, starting with their antiquarian Bibles.

No one should be publicly called a godparent anymore. The state would no longer recognize religious weddings as civil events, so the religious couple would have to have two ceremonies, as is done in France. There could be no state funerals, memorial services of days, or mourning from "national cathedrals." Military chaplains would need to be privatized because they are often on the public payroll. And all religious schools, healthcare institutions, social services, and Third World development agencies would be barred from receiving any state aid, no matter what good they do, because in a secular world it can't be supported if done in God's name. Consequently, the state would need to bear the burden of seeing a dramatic shrinkage of the biggest nongovernment provider of healthcare, welfare, and education in many countries. Sporting groups called the *demons, devils, saints, angels, friars, cardinals,* or *crusaders* may need a name change. Any Christian religious procession, a peal from the belfry, a call to prayer from a minaret, the blast of the shofar, and the ringing of the Buddhist *bonshō* and especially the enormous *ōgane* could be outlawed as civil disturbances. Finally, phrases with biblical and religious origins might have to be dropped like speaking of a "good Samaritan," a "prodigal son," a "doubting Thomas," or referring to a meal seemingly prepared from nowhere as the "loaves and the fish."

Does all this sound absurd? It could be. I hope it is. Earlier I admonished people who were theologically adolescent, all or nothing, and I also said that extreme cases do not prove principles, so I do not want to do either of those things here, except to say that in France, one of the most secular countries on earth, the burka has now been legally banned, and in the United Kingdom, Canada, and Italy there are legal cases against individuals wearing crosses and crucifixes in public. Furthermore, there has been fierce opposition to any religious symbols at the 9/11 memorial, which, especially for the families of the victims, is a monumental cemetery. It is, therefore, not so ridiculous to imagine that some of what we describe above could be outlawed because it offends secular sensibilities.

Unless radical atheists and secular humanists want to cherry-pick the bits of Christianity and other religious influences they like, then the denuded secular world just outlined is bleak. However, I am not on my own in thinking that the promised secular order would have its severe limitations. Andrew Murray writes,

> My fellow atheist opponents...portrayed the future—
> if we could only shrug off religion—as a wonderful
> sunlit upland, where reasonable people would make

reasonable decisions in a reasonable world. Is it not at least equally likely that if you keep telling people that they lead meaningless lives in a meaningless universe you might just find yourself with—at best—a vacuous life and a hollow culture? My first exhibit in submission involves turning on a television.[21]

More positively, I think Charles Taylor sums up the tension within which we now live in regard to the mixed history of religion in society and its undoubted accomplishments in Western culture.

It is reasonable to suppose that cultures that have provided the horizon of meaning for large numbers of human beings, of diverse characters and temperaments, over a long period of time—that have, in other words, articulated their sense of the good, the holy, the admirable—are almost certain to have something that deserves our admiration and respect even if it is accompanied by much that we have to abhor and reject.[22]

THE WORST ASPECT OF RELIGION IS ITS MORALIZING. HOW CAN SUCH OUTDATED THINKING OFFER ANYTHING TO MODERN SOCIETY?

Almost every major ethical and moral tradition has very ancient roots, so just because a way of thinking may have a long history, that does not make it obsolete. In fact, one of the things I like most about Christian ethics is its adaptability, because while human contexts change and develop, human nature remains a constant. Rather than talk about this in the abstract, I want to provide a case study of how relevant and liberating Christian morality can be to modern issues.

The Internet is now, arguably, one of the greatest developments in recent centuries. Its potential for good and ill is well documented. Applying some of the Christian morality outlined above, our first response to the Internet is entirely positive. Christians are not against everything. As St. Thomas Aquinas says, wherever there is justice, temperance, fortitude, prudence, mercy, and hospitality then God is present—and these virtues can be found everywhere online.[23]

We also know, however, that the seven deadly sins are also alive and well online. One of the worst choices we can make online is to use this technology to bully others. There are presently scores of legal cases in every OECD country calling citizens to account for what they have written online. Though they are entitled to their opinions, not all opinions are of equal value, and ones that defame, especially anonymously, are immoral. Gossip, deliberate misrepresentation, character assassination, and libel are not about knowledge. They are about power, and there seems to be plenty of abuse of it occurring online. Apart from the Lord's golden rule, "Do unto others as you would have them do unto you," a further clarifying question to ask is this: Is what I am about to say, blog, or post kind? That does not mean we do not post tough ideas and thoughts online or engage in robust debate. It is just that, as in all correspondence, we should speak the truth as we see it in charity. The tougher the line we want to post, the more charitable a way we should find to say it.

The issue of cyberbullying leads to a more general problem of privacy. Whatever else the mobile phone and social networking sites have done in the Western world, they have changed the nature of privacy. These days, many of us have been forced to listen to excruciating and sometimes sensitive or potentially defamatory conversations by a mobile phone user. Frequently on social networking sites, people can tell too much of their story too quickly, and post images that would be better left in a more private sphere. This is part of what psychologists call inappropriate disclosure that relates to the time and place, the depth and content, and to whom we are disclosing. As Christians, we are all called to be prudent, which in this context indicates that meaningful and deep relationships often take time. The sharing of our stories requires a safe environment where our history will be respected. We also need to be certain that the story we post online is ours to tell. It is unethical to disclose to anyone else details about others' lives for which we do not have their permission to share. Before posting something online, it is often helpful to ask yourself this question: "Would I stand up and tell a large crowd of strangers what I am about to post?" If not, then chances are you should not write it online, because you are potentially telling the world.

An associated ethical disconnect in the area of digital privacy is the disempowerment of parents in regard to the supervision of their children in the home. The youngster's digital technology can be seen as "private" and parents as having no rights to access it. With an OECD family size average of 1.9 children living in a house with 3.7 bedrooms, the relatively new phenomenon of single occupancy bedrooms with locked doors changes the role and scope of parental digital supervision. Theoretically, uninvited strangers are visiting homes every day without the parents' knowledge.

A related issue of ethics and culture in the digital sphere relates to the concept of reality. Some people create new personae for themselves online. The mediated self cannot meet cyber friends because the created person is false. The split between the created online self and the real self can have significantly dangerous implications for adolescent mental health. Connected studies are also looking at the real versus the idealized self, where a person may invent or exaggerate attributes, gifts, talents, or physical traits.

Some social networking sites aid and abet the creation of a person who may not exist, or at least not in the form assumed. Significant psychological conflict comes from the greatest separation of the idealized and realized self, especially if the created persona is in direct conflict with the values, attitudes, and practices of the real self. Though this can be seen as an act of imagination or being an actor online, we are starting to see how this technology maldevelops some at-risk young adults.

A related ongoing issue is the relatively new phenomenom

of what is now termed the *techno addict*. Last year, the Illinois Institute for Addiction Recovery accepted technology as fulfilling all the requirements of a diagnosis of addiction, along with alcohol, drugs, sex, gambling, work, food, and shopping.

Some people are now compulsive about sending and receiving emails, making multiple visits on any day to social networking sites, having access to a mobile phone at all times, resulting in personal, family, academic, financial, and occupational problems characteristic of other addictions: impairment of real life relationships; secrecy becoming paramount; personal and social withdrawal; deceit; and an excessive interest in violent material.

Staying with online violence for a moment, the debated research of Oxford University neuropharmacologist Baroness Susan Greenfield presents some interesting conclusions: "It's pretty clear that the screen-based, two dimensional world that so many teenagers—and a growing number of adults—choose to inhabit is producing changes in behaviour. Attention spans are shorter, personal communication skills are reduced and there's a marked reduction in the ability to think abstractly."[24] Her research into young adults addicted to violent computer games concludes that while there is no evidence they perpetrate violent acts at a higher rate, when confronted with real-life violence they demonstrate a significantly different response in regard to empathy and sensitivity.

Another online addiction, of course, is the dehumanizing world of pornography, combining as it does a perfect storm of two addictions: sex and technology. There is a spirited debate about the size and profitability of online pornography. We do know that in 2013 there were seven million pornographic domain name sites, thirteen thousand X-rated films were released, and that sixty-eight million requests were made for pornographic websites across the major search engines. Estimates of the annual worth of pornography varies anywhere from $1.5 billion to $4.9 billion. What we also know is that successive government inquiries in many countries have found that organized crime and drug industries were major stakeholders in and producers of online pornography. In the United States last year, phone sex generated $4.5 billion in sales[25] and "sexting" is now a very serious issue. It is no respecter of educational or ethnic background, social class, zip codes, or, as sadly we have to publicly own, being a believer or not, or being a Christian layperson or a cleric. Gail Dines shows how pornography is also becoming more violent, degrading, and sadistically misogynistic.[26]

What's our Christian ethical response? Morally, we believe that our sexuality is a gift given by God to be enjoyed, nurtured, and developed, but that we also stand against anything that reduces sex to a commodity we trade for fun or favors. The key word for Christian sexual morality is *dignity*—for myself, for others, and even for those who may not claim it for themselves.

Adapting Canadian Jesuit John Pungente's helpful tool outlined in *Media Literacy: A Resource Guide*, we can begin to see how our understanding of morality may stem from a long tradition, but that it still assists, counsels, guides, and supports us in being ethical online and consuming it wisely. Pugente outlines the EABV model: *event, attitude, behavior,* and *values.*[27]

Event. While we often focus on what we take away from the Internet, it is also helpful to analyze what we take to it in the first place. If we take boredom, we will "surf," watching anything to kill time. If we take loneliness, then we might end up sharing too much about ourselves to strangers. If we take arousal, then guess which websites we go to? What we take away from Internet is defined in part by what we bring to it.

Attitude. There is no such thing as a value-neutral Internet site. What is not included or is taken out and not explored is often more revealing than what the site does present. Ethical consumers try to understand what the Internet makers are communicating by being alert to the side of the story that is not told.

Behavior. Increasingly, producers of Internet sites simply want us to buy stuff—and lots of it. Large-scale advertising campaigns, product placement, merchandise tie-ins, goods, and services are all commodities up for grabs. Critical consumers are also aware of the intellectual property being sold in the Internet marketplace. These days, a product or an idea rarely makes an appearance without paying to be there.

Values. Applying the values test to the Internet means asking if the story, theme, and atmosphere of the site are consistent with faith, hope, and love. How does this online product enable the "fruit of the Spirit" (Gal 5:22)—joy, peace, patience, kindness, goodness, fidelity, gentleness, and self-control—to grow in me? It may emphasize one of these values over the others, but if it does not include any of them, then chances are it is a site that cannot be reconciled with our Christian values.

Moral behavior online means that we commit to promoting an online culture of respect, dialogue, and friendship; to valuing life not just as a succession of events or experiences, but a search for the true, the good, and the beautiful; and to believing that the digital community should be accessible to those who are already economically and socially marginalized, and not contributing to the increasing gap between the world's rich and poor.

Finally, I think we should all become good storytellers. Christians are not the enemies of fun and surely some element of the online world is just about entertainment. Life does not have to be deadly dull and serious all the time. Some Internet sites are just about telling stories, fictional and real. The most important lessons can be learned through stories—while people are laughing, crying, being confronted, and consoled. However, while the online world is an important part of our world, we know that away from our computers our lives are of greater value because we are living our lives. Our lives matter more than anything else.

CONCLUSION

In practicing what I preach, let me tell you a story about venturing to what was, for me, a foreign land and finding amazing grace.

In December 1993, immediately after being ordained, I was appointed as the assistant priest at St. Canice's, the Catholic parish of King's Cross—the "red light" district of Sydney. It was, as you could imagine, a very colorful parish.

Soon after my ordination, I went to Queensland to say Masses at the Catholic schools, parishes, and communities to which I had belonged over the years at Warwick, Toowoomba, and Brisbane. I returned to King's Cross on Christmas Eve and was told by my seventy-year-old Irish parish priest that I would be presiding at Midnight Mass. What he did not tell me is that while I was away, Esme, our eighty-year-old sacristan, had gone all over to buy every meter of gold lamé in Sydney that there was to buy to make me a set of vestments for the occasion.

I saw it for the first time when I arrived into the sacristy. Of course, I had to wear it and when I put it on and looked in the mirror, with Esme beaming beside me, I looked like a bloody Christmas tree: wrap lights around me and plug me in and I would have flashed—though not literally!

Midnight Mass was packed to the rafters and, by the way this Catholic congregation sang, it was fairly clear that most people were full of more than one type of Christmas cheer!

Soon after Mass began, five tall men in white blouson shirts walked all the way down the aisle to the only available seat in the church—the very front pew. It was clear that only one of them knew what to do at Mass. He instructed the others to stand, kneel, sit, roll over, and die. (All the things we do at Mass—and we do, in a sense, die with Christ in the Eucharist.)

After Mass, at drinks on the footpath, I went over to these men and welcomed them to the parish. "Hello, I'm Fr. Richard Leonard. I haven't seen you here before and I'd like to wish you a very Happy Christmas." To which one of the five turned to me and said, "Father, if you don't mind me saying so, you wear your frock divinely." At that moment, I turned into the butchest priest in Australia. "I don't get any kicks out of wearing this stuff you know. I normally get straight back to the sacristy and take it off." And as soon I said that, I really wished I hadn't.

It transpired that my five new parishioners were from the now-defunct *Les Girls Show*. They were at 2 Roslyn Street for twenty-nine years. St. Canice's is at 28 Roslyn St. That night they had done the usual show at 10:30 p.m., but, as a Christmas special, they still had a late, late show to do at 3:00 a.m. Mark, the only Catholic among them, had convinced his colleagues to "get some religion and come to Midnight Mass."

They had enjoyed Mass so much that Mark suggested that I get a few of the other Jesuits and come up the hill at 3:00 a.m. "Seeing that we came to your show, Father, you should come to ours." I declined the offer, but Mark explained that, in case I changed my mind, there would be tickets waiting for me at the door.

As they were about to walk up the hill, the one who told me that I wore my frock divinely said to me, "Father if ever you want some help to tizz up any of your little church outfits, just let me know, because I am a wonderful designer, and I know I could do a number on you." At that moment, I had visions of coming out from the sacristy the following week in plums, feathers, and a tiara.

When I got back to the presbytery, I told three young visiting Jesuit students the entire story. It transpired that none of us had been to *Les Girls*. Guess what happened next?

We were late for their show, too, but the tickets were waiting for us at the door, there was a table at the back, which suited me just fine, and we were served complimentary drinks. To my relief, no one had seen us enter and I decided we would be leaving early as well. St. Ignatius has lots to say about things done in the dark—but we won't go there for the moment.

The girls put on a great show and everything was going along quite nicely until at the end. Mark, now in his Marcia persona, went to the microphone to wish everyone a Happy Christmas. He told the audience that to celebrate Christmas the girls had been to Midnight Mass in between the late shows and that as a result of that "we'd like to welcome our local Catholic clergy." With that announcement, a spotlight came on our table! I stood and waved to all my new parishioners.

Marcia then told the crowd that I had sung at Midnight Mass and invited me to "come up here on stage to lead the crowd in a rousing chorus of 'O come, all ye faithful.'" As I walked to the stage, all I could think of was how I am going to explain this to the cardinal, my Irish Jesuit parish priest, my provincial Superior (who now happens to be our rector), or worst of all, my mother when she found out!

Do you have any idea who goes to the late, late show of *Les Girls* on Christmas morning—that is, other than young Jesuits!? But there I was, not three weeks ordained, at 4:30 a.m. on the stage of *Les Girls* at King's Cross, leading a very dubious group of our compatriots in singing, "O come let us adore him, Christ the Lord."

Within six months of that night, I had buried three of the five men who came to Midnight Mass. One suicided in March. We had to break into his apartment in Darlinghurst to find him and the gun. The second man died of a heroin overdose in St. Canice's public toilets. I found him dead in the cubicle when I was locking up. The last man died of HIV/AIDS in the Sisters of Charity hospice in June.

After his mates died, the fourth man wanted to get out of King's Cross and start a new life. We helped him reestablish himself in rural New South Wales. I baptized him at St. Canice's in 1994. I did his wedding there in 2000. I received his wife into the Catholic Church in 2002, and the following year, at the only church they knew and liked, I baptized their triplets. Mark, the only Catholic on that first night at the church, now works full time with homeless teenagers in Sydney. He was once homeless himself, being ordered out of his family home at sixteen, when he told his parents that he thought he was gay. He and his partner remain devout parishioners of another inner city Sydney Catholic parish.

Now, there are some Catholics and Christians who think that those "entertainment workers" should never have fronted up to Midnight Mass. They would most certainly believe that the Jesuits had no place ever going to *Les Girls* that night, of all nights, if any night. However, on both scores they are utterly wrong. The reason Christ and the church touched these men's lives for the better was not just because they came to us, as good as that was, but that we got off our backsides and went to them where they were, and met them as they were.

In doing so, we formed a relationship with them that gave two of them options they and we could never have dreamed about for their lives that first night, and, at least for the other three, they received the dignity of a Christian burial, which I think is a dignity always worth having.

Our Christian ethical behavior is always in context and it connects our real lives with others so that we might be the best people we can be. At its best, it is never moralizing, but allows a tradition with ancient roots of reflecting on human nature for two thousand years to adapt it to the here and now. I find that liberating.

Chapter Three

WITNESSES OF FAITH, HOPE, AND LOVE

The most eloquent argument in support of belief is not what we say, but what we do. In this chapter, we will outline the lives of several saints, canonized or otherwise, some heroic Christians, and great human beings who have inspired me. For while Judaism has Hebrew as its sacred language, and Islam has Arabic, it is the body, the flesh, that is the sacred language of Christianity.[1]

These people are not just good people. They are most certainly that, but they did or do what they do, not only and simply because of their love for humanity, but also because of their love of God: Father, Son, and Spirit.

We mostly hear about believers who betray us by their criminally destructive behavior, rather than about the vast majority who quietly and powerfully walk the talk. While we have to judge the terrible choices some Christians have made and the shocking fallout that their behavior has had on others, we cannot condemn them. Condemnation is for God alone who knows all, sees all, and is justice itself. Our worst sinners no more define us as believers than the worst of any group defines that group. Most Christian believers, though fragile and sinful, make our world a better place every single day by their faith, hope, and love. Clearly, we do not have the morality market captured, for apart from our notorious sinners, there are millions of people who reject faith and live lives of heroic goodness. Some of the more famous outstanding secular organizations that come to mind in this regard are the Red Cross, Red Crescent, UNICEF, Doctors Without Borders/Médecins Sans

Frontières, the United Nations High Commission for Refugees, Amnesty International, Oxfam, CARE, Save the Children, and the United Nations Office for the Coordination of Humanitarian Affairs. Our world would be impoverished by their absence.

As much as possible, these pen pictures of saints will not go over old ground. I want to provide an insight into some people who are widely loved by many, some of whom you may not have heard about before or whose lives you have not reflected upon for a while. In each case, it is my hope to provide a new window or insight into their lives, sometimes use a film to observe their witness, and draw out contemporary lessons from how they lived out their faith.

ST. THOMAS MORE (1478–1535)

Hilary Mantel won many awards for her novel *Wolf Hall* about the fortunes of the Seymour family in England from 1500 to 1535. It is beautifully written and wonderfully researched, but Thomas More should sue for defamation. At Mantel's hands, More is not *A Man for All Seasons*, a phrase used by Robert Bolt as the title for his play and film but coined by More's contemporary, Robert Whittington in 1522: "More is a man of an angel's wit and singular learning…a man of marvelous mirth and pastimes, and sometime of as sad gravity. A man for all seasons." In Mantel's hands, More is only a man of deepest winter, a religious zealot responsible for many more deaths in God's name than his own. Fortunately for Thomas's memory, Mantel's account of him owes more to the portrait of a contemporary religious suicide bomber than to a complex Renaissance man whose own son-in-law, William Roper, wrote the first laudatory biography about him, and this in honor of the man who left the family broke, disgraced, and in personal danger! I know whose judgment I think is closer to the actual subject.

Thomas More was indeed a complex man. He was twice married, first to Jane Colt in 1505. They had four children. When Jane died in 1511 he remarried, this time to a widow named Alice Middleton, who had a daughter from her first marriage.

Thomas and Alice never had any children of their own. Sadly and revealingly, it is rare enough for a married man to be canonized a Catholic saint, but to be seemingly happily married twice, and, after everything you put them through, to have the lifelong devotion of your children and even your in-laws is in itself a miracle.

More's story is familiar. King Henry VIII of England wanted to divorce his wife, the devoutly Catholic Catherine of Aragon. The pope would not dissolve the bond, so Henry worked to end the pope's authority over the church in England, which eventually became the Church of England. To do this, Henry needed the approval of the peers and the parliament. The king regarded his chancellor, Sir Thomas More, as a loyal friend. However, by 1530, Henry required that the English clergy take oaths of allegiance to him as "Supreme Head of the Church of England." Not long after, Thomas More resigned his post. When Henry insisted that all peers sign the Act of Succession—recognizing his powers over church and state, as well as his new marriage—More refused. In 1535, he was tried, found guilty of treason, and beheaded.

Although Bolt deserved all the awards he won for his play and film, *A Man for All Seasons*, the last third of this work was not primarily written by Bolt. It is a masterful editing of the actual transcripts of the trial of Thomas More, who in today's terms was England's prime minister. The trial lasted one day—July 1, 1535—within Westminster Hall. The outcome of the jury's fifteen-minute deliberations were never in doubt. To have found More not guilty would have incurred Henry's wrath, so it was a show trial in every sense.

The Duke of Norfolk then offered More a final chance to escape with his life: "You see now how grievously you have offended his Majesty; yet he is so very merciful that if you will lay aside your obstinacy, and change your opinion, we hope you may obtain pardon and favor in his sight." More replied—"stoutly," according to reports—that he appreciated the offer, "but I beseech Almighty God that I may continue in the mind I am in, through his grace, unto death."[2]

More said in his defense that, when the king asked him for his opinion about the divorce, he said that the state has no authority to dissolve the marriage. Stating the truth of the law, he contended, can hardly be treasonous. The Duke of Norfolk said, "Thomas, look at these names! Why can't you do as I did and come with us, for fellowship?" "And when we die," More replied, "and you are sent to heaven for doing your conscience, and I am sent to hell for not doing mine, will you come with me, for fellowship?"

Thomas More was found guilty and sentenced to be "drawn on a hurdle through the City of London to Tyburn, there to be hanged till he should be half dead; then he should be cut down alive, his privy parts cut off, his belly ripped, his bowels burnt, his four quarters sit up over four gates of the City and his head upon London Bridge." Henry VIII had this commuted to a simple beheading.

Of the many modern lessons from St. Thomas More's witness to belief, two stand out: the importance of silence, and being prepared to die rather than wanting to be killed.

In every account of Jesus' trial, he hardly says a word before his accuser and yet his silence is deafening. Thomas More learned from Jesus that standing up to the crowd who want you to compromise your conscience starts with silence. All believers are called to be contemplatives in action, praying for the courage to dissent from the crowd's hyped-up madness. In a world where we have never communicated more, are we listening? Thomas More reminds us that there is a time to speak and a time to be quiet. It starts with silence. He wrote in his breviary:

> Give me the grace good Lord,
> to set the world at naught;
> to set my mind fast upon Thee
> and not to hang upon the blast of men's mouths.
> To be content to be solitary...
> To bear the cross with Christ,
> To have the last thing—death—in remembrance.

Thomas More did not want to die. He was not the sixteenth-century version of a suicide bomber that Hilary Mantel makes him. Christian martyrs do not seek death, but will go to death for the sake of their faith in Christ, their informed conscience, and the struggle for justice that the cause of right always involves. More's martyrdom involved his faith, conscience, and justice. More knew that betraying his principles and values would cause a dying with which he could not live. He ended his life with simple eloquence: "I am commanded by the king to be brief, and since I am the king's obedient subject, brief I will be. I die His Majesty's good servant, but God's first."

ST. IGNATIUS LOYOLA (1491–1556)

Name changes are significant in the Bible. The most famous ones in the Old Testament are Abram to Abraham, Sarai to Sarah, and Jacob to Israel. In the New Testament, only two people have name changes: Simon to Peter, and Saul to Paul. They indicate a turning around of one's life after a commissioning by God. Some Catholic religious men and most religious women used to take on the name of a patron saint when they entered convents as a mark of the change in their life. Since 1009, on being elected into office, almost all popes have done it too, though John XII (955–64), Benedict IX (1032–48), Boniface VIII (1294–1303), Clement VI (1342–52), Sixtus IV (1471–84), Innocent VIII (1484–92), Alexander VI (1492–1503), Julius II (1503–13), and Julius III (1550–55) should not have bothered with the name change, because the only difference we can find in their behavior was that each one became demonstrably worse afterward.

The now St. Ignatius of Loyola was born in the Basque region of northern Spain in 1491. We know from family records that he was baptized Iñigo Lopez de Oñaz y Loyola after St. Enecus (Innicus), Abbot of Oña. He changed his name himself in Paris, around forty-one years later, to Ignatius in honor of the early martyr St. Ignatius of Antioch. His name change chartered an extraordinary journey he had both completed and upon which he was just embarking: from soldier to saint, from philanderer to founder, and from masochist to mystic.

Does the first part of the last category sound harsh? I may be the only Jesuit who will tell you this, but St. Ignatius was also an obsessive, compulsive, neurotic nut. That's not fair, of course, because he was also a genuinely holy, mystical, and brilliant man of his time, but some of his behavior can easily lead us to conclude that my comment is neither facetious nor unwarranted. In fact, one of the most important chapters in his life gives the key to why Ignatian spirituality has been so enduring and adaptable. I want take you to the cave at Manresa in 1522, where Ignatius had his best and worst days. Ignatius dictated an autobiography, and we know from it and from letters he later wrote that it was in that cave that his Rules for the Discernment of Spirits, arguably his greatest gift to the Church, were formed. That cave was also the scene of some very dangerous behavior.

We know that on the way to the abbey on Montserrat—from where he left for Manresa—he encountered a Muslim man who defamed the Virgin Mary. Iñigo was so offended he wanted to kill him, but he could not decide whether to do it or not. Just ahead there was a fork in the road, so he let the reins on his donkey go loose, and if the donkey chose to go the same way as the Muslim, he decided he would murder him. If it took the other path, he would not. Thank God the donkey had more sense than Iñigo! In the cave, we know that Ignatius, the penitent, whipped himself three times a day for months, wore an iron girdle, fasted on bread and water for which he begged, slept very little and only then on the ground, spent up to seven hours on his knees at prayer, covered his face with dirt, grew his hair and beard rough, and allowed his dirty nails to grow to a grotesque length. We also know that he suffered from spiritual scruples so badly that he considered committing suicide by throwing himself into the River Cardonner. We would now diagnose the Ignatius of 1522 as being an at-risk self-harmer suffering from an acute depressive disorder exhibiting suicidal behavior.

Two things saved him. First, because he was a soldier, he

was used to taking orders from legitimate authorities and following them. Second, he believed in the wisdom of the Church. When his Dominican confessor at Manresa saw how far Ignatius was deteriorating mentally and spiritually, he ordered him, under holy obedience, to eat food, wash, cut his hair and nails, stop the penances, and take care of himself. Ignatius had to obey. From there, Ignatius turned a corner and emerged a wise and holy man. Manresa changed him forever. Not just because he had undergone these terrible experiences and lived to tell the tale, but because he *reflected carefully* on how good things like prayer, penance, and fasting can quickly become instruments of self-destruction, even in the name of God.

The life of Ignatius appeals to anyone who has glimpsed a very dark place and has needed to find a way back from that abyss. His wisdom in regard to the careful discernment of spirits was won in the face of staring down some very destructive demons indeed. What is best about the insights of Ignatius is how practical they are. In modern parlance, we would now say Ignatius encourages us to "keep it real."

Ignatius says the spiritual quest starts with our desires, asking, "What do I really want in my life?" Our desires are pivotal to our search. We often look for all the right things in all the wrong places, and some pay for it for the rest of their lives. Unlike what many people think today, Ignatius would not rate "being happy" as the most important desire to have and possess. Not that he was against joy. He was not a member of the fun police. In fact, Ignatius was famous for his sense of humor and he loved a party. It is just that he would argue against what we sometimes hear parents say they want for their children: "I don't care what my kids do, as long as they're happy"; or we might say, "I need to make some big changes in my life because I should be happier." Maybe we need to make some big changes in our life, but not for the primary pursuit of happiness. In this world, everlasting happiness is a myth. Ignatius knew that.

The social researcher, Hugh Mackay, sums up our contemporary problem with happiness being the essential human goal:

Weekends should be great....Holidays should be havens of happiness....Work should be fun, or, if not fun, then at least stimulating and satisfying. So should marriage, and if it isn't, then we should strive for a perfect divorce in which we and our former partner will behave in the civilised and responsible way we couldn't quite manage during the marriage....The kids themselves should be gifted in ways that make them worthy of special attention.....*Our* counsellors, it goes without saying, should be gurus....Sex should be blissful and deeply satisfying, every time....Sport? It's all about winning, of course....Our cars should be perfectly safe....The state should leave us alone to get on with our lives in peace but should exert tight control over the behaviour of other people who mightn't be as responsible or competent as we are....In our perfect world, blame is easy to affix, revenge is sweet, and outcomes are always positive (for us). Life should proceed from one thrilling gratification to the next, banners triumphantly aflutter, joy unbounded. All we want is heaven on earth. Is that too much to ask?[3]

When he emerged from the darkness of that cave, Ignatius knew that happiness would be the welcome byproduct of living out the highest goals in life: to be the most loving, hopeful, and faithful person possible. How would people respond if we were to make that response our new mantra to the question, What to do you most want for your kids? "I really just want them to be the most faithful, hopeful, and loving people they can be." As in everything important in their lives, our children and young adults would learn what this looks like from the adult role models around them.

For the last thirty-two years of his life, Ignatius moved away from trying to find the easy side of easy, to embodying Jesus' call to love God, his neighbor, and himself. He knew that learning from hard-won lessons, confronting tough moments, and embracing suffering were inescapable and important moments in coming to grips with our human condition. He also knew that, when we try to do this on our own, we can be defeated by isolation and fear. That is why he put such store in the community of faith, the church, because he knew we needed each other and that God was found in the midst of companionship, of being "friends in the Lord."

Consequently, Ignatius thought the task of life was to be as reflective as possible—"a contemplative in action"—so as to discern the patterns that lead us to be more hopeful, faithful, and loving, and to learn those patterns that lead us to being less so. Ignatius knew that most positive and negative things in our life don't just happen. He believed very strongly in habits, in building on the good ones and working against the bad. This means constantly assessing the what, and why, of our decisions.

Ignatius also knew that, before we come to make a decision, we need to address the three big blocks in most people's lives that can blind us from a range of choices: riches, pride, and honor. From his own experience and in accompanying many others in their spiritual search, he knew that these vices entrapped people.

Riches are not just about money, but the enticement of material wealth as well as physical beauty, intellectual prowess, reputation, status, and power. It all centered on who possessed whom or what. Ignatius was once incredibly vain in the pursuit of worldly wealth and status for its own sake. It was a dead end for him and he suggests it is for all of us. He also argued that riches lead to honor, where we want to be acclaimed and praised all the time, and we expect that life will be easier because of our wealth and power. This is not new. Seneca, a second-century philosopher, noted in his book on anger how the richest people he knew also seemed to be the angriest because they thought their money would buy them an easier life in every way. When it didn't, they became angry. Furthermore, riches and honor lead to pride where we have to be like God—always in charge. Today, we would call proud people, in the sense that Ignatius uses the term, control freaks, trying to control everyone and everything for their benefit, or to their will. For Ignatius, the spiritual quest is about staring down the seductive side of these things and reclaiming wealth, beauty, status, intellect, and power as gifts given by God to be used for the coming of Christ's kingdom. Note that he did not reject these elements in our lives. He was smarter than that. He recrafts them for higher and better purposes.

Ignatius thought that in the spiritual life there are three types of people: the first is the one who lives from desire to desire, not caring about God one way or another; the second is the person who wants to attend to their spiritual journey but their bad habits, negative attitudes, and vanity get in the road of making much progress; the last type is the one whose genuine desire is to follow God and live a life of faith, hope, and love. Rather than a type of person, each is a stage, through which we all too often move in and out of, and backward and forward.

To keep the momentum going in the right direction, Ignatius encourages us to deepen our humility. The spiritual concept of humility has had a bad rap. It does not mean feeling bad about oneself. The word comes from the Latin, *humus*, meaning "close to the earth," and a good way to start being truly humble is to fight against a sense of entitlement and simply be grateful for everything. We did not create the world; we inherited it and, as a start, that should make us profoundly grateful. Keep it real! Ignatius thought there were three degrees of humility: the first degree is found in a person who lives a good life so as to attain heaven; the second degree is a person who lives a good life in order to bring faith, hope, and love to bear in our world in a way that liberates others as it has liberated themselves; finally, there are those who want to be like Christ in every way, serving the poor and being a prophet, and prepared to take rejection and insults so as to point to a greater love.

There is great symbolism in a name change. Ignatius went from being a vain, violent, but aimless egotist to knowing that the desire to be a faithful, hopeful, and loving follower of Christ was the best way to live. His conversion is enshrined in his "Prayer for Generosity":[4]

Take hold of me Lord.
Accept this offering of freedom, of memory, of mind, of
    will.
These I cling and count as my own.
All are your gifts, Lord, now I am returning them.
They are yours. Do as you will.
Give me only your free gift of love.
In this you give all; in this you give all.

VENERABLE CATHERINE MCAULEY (1778–1841)

The stories of many Catholic women religious founders are inspiring: Catherine McAuley, Mary Ward, Nano Nagle, and Mary Aitkenhead, just to name a few. Catherine was the foundress of the Sisters of Mercy. This quartet of pioneering women had to put up with what we now call overt sexism and blatant discrimination, and much of it done in the name of God and the Church. However, while these women's detractors are now forgotten to history, each of them is on the road to being declared a saint, and rightly so.

The Sisters of Mercy who taught me were important in forming my admiration for their foundress. In fact, my admiration started even before that. My mother was a nun, or at least she was a Sister of Mercy for twenty-three months. I have a photo to prove it! Dated January 22, 1955, the happy snapshot is of Sister Mary Thérèsia on her reception day. A freshly minted bride of Christ, she had just had her hair cut off and was now bedecked in all the regalia the nuns used to wear. By 1957, she had fled the convent. That is not an exaggeration. My mother literally ran away late one Sunday afternoon, and the only thing she took with her was an old Latin prayer book and that photograph of herself as a nun. As a little boy, I found that prayer book at home and the photograph within it. I can remember thinking, "Who is that nun who looks a bit like Mum?" A few years later, I dared to ask. Although it was a minor local Catholic scandal in its day, thank God she left the Mercies or I would not be here as I am. Nevertheless, that's where my devotion to Mother McAuley began. My school was an extension of my home.

Like my mother, Catherine McAuley also did a few things that raised Catholic eyebrows. By the time Catherine was twenty, she was an orphan—her father died when she was five and her mother passed away in 1798. Desperately poor, the three surviving McAuley children went to live with their mother's cousin, William Armstrong. He was a very committed Protestant who tried to get the children to join the Church of Ireland. Two of them did convert, but Catherine, the eldest, was resolutely against it. Five years later, she went into the full-time service of a Quaker couple, William and Catherine Callaghan. Miss McAuley was Mrs Callaghan's live-in caretaker until the older lady's death in 1819, by which time, through Catherine's influence and example, she had become a Catholic. Catherine then cared for William until his death in 1822. He made a deathbed conversion as well.

Late conversions notwithstanding, maybe only in Northern Ireland today is it still possible to imagine the suspicion that would have surrounded a Catholic woman living with Protestants for twenty-four years. The childless Mr. Callaghan bequeathed his whole and substantial estate to Catherine McAuley.

At forty-four, rather than live the life of an heiress, Catherine wanted to do something for the poor women and children of Dublin. On the Feast of Our Lady of Mercy, September 24, 1827, the House of Mercy on Baggot Street, Dublin, was opened for the education, feeding, clothing, housing, safe haven, and basic healthcare of girls, women, and their children.

Against her first desire, but to protect her work, Catherine McAuley, Mary Ann Doyle, and Mary Elizabeth Harley professed their religious vows as the first Sisters of Mercy on December 12, 1831. Catherine died on November 11, 1841, aged sixty-three, at which time there were Mercy convents throughout Ireland and England—a hundred women had joined her. Fourteen years later, there were three thousand Sisters of Mercy. Today, there are around nine thousand "Mercies" working for the poor and needy in education, healthcare, social services, spirituality, pastoral care, and in advocacy for women, children, and refugees.

When my mother, the former Sister Mary Thérèsia, RSM, came to visit me in London in 1997, she wanted to go to Ireland to visit our family and friends there, and to see the new International Mercy Centre at Baggot Street, Dublin. She had been told by a former fellow Mercy sister that she had seen her own name in the "Mercy Book," wherein are recorded the names of every woman who has entered the sisters anywhere in the world.

Our visit to Ireland did not start well. My mother fell and broke her ankle within four hours of arriving at the airport. Pressing on, but now in a cast, two days later we decided to visit Baggot Street. Mary Goggins, a great Irish friend of ours, led the way. A lifelong friend of mine from home, Christopher Perkins, who was visiting Dublin at the same time, decided to tag along. An excellent communicator and former journalist, Christopher has a questioning mind about everything—religious faith in general, and saints in particular.

Having asked ahead, we knew the last tour of Baggot Street was conducted at 2 p.m. and that it finished with a "comfortable cup of tea." Finding an accessible car park was the first challenge. My mother negotiating her way to the door on crutches was the second one. We arrived in the foyer at 2:05 p.m. The tour had left. Mary must have known that we might have needed some insurance, because that day she told me to wear my clerical collar. I did. When the Sister of Mercy at the reception desk would not let us catch up to the departed tour, Mary swung into action. She had been taught by the Mercies at Cahirciveen, County Kerry. She had Sister's measure: "Sister, Father Leonard's mother was not in the country five minutes when she fell and broke her leg. She has come all the way from Australia just to see Mother Catherine's tomb and it would break her heart not to do so." It was a bit of an overstatement, but it worked. Sister took a look at my mother's cast and then my clerical collar and relented. We caught the lift to the second floor and joined the tour just as it entered the most important room in the building: Mother Catherine McAuley's bedroom. We were all made "very, very welcome."

Our tour leader was an Irish Sister who gave us a vivid pen picture of Mother Catherine and the significance of the room we were now in. She said, "You are standing in the very room where Mother Catherine decided to found the Sisters of Mercy…and this is the very desk at which she wrote the Constitutions…and that is the very bed upon which she died." Our touring party was humbled to be in such a sacred place. Some were moved to tears.

When Sister had finished her moving commentary, my mother, noticing on the wall the famous portrait of Catherine McAuley at her desk, a replica of which hangs in every Mercy institution in the world, looked up at it and said, "Well, when I was a girl and in trouble with nuns, I certainly did time under that painting, being told to ask for Mother Catherine's help." The tour now started to fall apart. "Well," said our tour guide in her educated Dublin accent, "that's really not Mother Catherine. No, she was too humble to sit for her portrait while she was alive, so after she died the sisters said to Mother Bridget, 'You look an awful lot like Mother Catherine, so you sit for the portrait,' and that's what happened."

Moved by the foundress's humility, Christopher reassured the silenced group, "Well, at least that's the very desk Mother Catherine used." "Well, maybe it's not the very desk," said Sister, "because there was a terrible fire here in 1884 and though everything was rebuilt, we lost a lot too." Christopher could now smell a story. "So if there was a fire this may not be the actual bed in which she died." "Well, it's very much like it," Sister said, a little sheepishly. Christopher knew he was on to something now. "So, we are not in the actual room, are we, because the actual room was burned out in the fire?" "Well, in general you might be right, but the place was rebuilt, you see, and we're very close to where Mother Catherine's actual room would have been." Now Perkins went in for the killer scoop: "So, Sister, we're not in the very room, that's not the actual desk, this is not the very bed, and that's not a portrait of Mother McAuley." "Yes," replied Sister, "that's technically right...because Mother was so humble she wouldn't sit for a portrait," and with that led the tour hastily out of the room of disputed claims.

Mary Goggins then produced an Irish five punt note, which, in those days, had Mother Catherine's portrait on it (this was before the Euro), and said in desperation, "So can anyone tell me who the hell this is?" To which the chorus of typically irreverent Australians said, "It's Mother Bridget!"

As we staggered into the corridor, Mary and my mother collapsed onto a pew in spasms of laughter. Chris and I caught up to the group, not wanting to miss a single minute in the next extraordinary installment of the most entertaining tour we had been on in years. As we arrived, Sister said to me, "Father, is your mother not coming along now?" And with that the group looked back to see Mary and my mother doubled over with their heads in their hands. From a distance, because the actions of laughing and crying can sometimes be hard to distinguish, Sister was convinced that the women in our party were moved to tears. "It happens often enough," she said sympathetically. "Mother Catherine's room has that effect on some pilgrims. We'll leave them be." And with that Sister asked the tour group to "look down and see Mother Catherine's mausoleum." Christopher immediately piped up from the back and asked affectionately, "Sister, are you sure?" "Oh yes, the fire didn't get that far," and on we went.

After my mother and Mary recovered from their attack of profound spiritual consolation, Chris and I were reunited with them in the Mercy Room wherein the Mercy Books reside. We found the Brisbane Congregation of the Sisters of Mercy and eagerly searched for the entry: "Helen Joan Davis, Sister Mary Thérèsia, 1955." We looked, and looked again, and looked a third time. The entries stopped in 1954. Sister explained, "Well Brisbane mustn't have updated us yet with their records beyond 1954. We've entered whatever we've received from them." It was then that my mother remembered that the fellow former Mercy sister who had told her about the book had entered the year before my mother, in 1954. Mary and my mother were overcome with another bout of profound spiritual consolation!

Meanwhile, Chris and I went and watched the documentary about how "Mercy went all over the world." Beautifully produced, it told the story of young women in the nineteenth century who left their parents, families, and home, never to return, and embarked on a boat to serve the poor all over the world in England (1839), Canada (1842), the United States of America (1843), Australia (1846), Scotland (1847), New Zealand (1850), to nurse in the Crimean War (1854), Belize (1883), British Guiana (1894), South Africa (1897), as well as throughout Ireland. As the lights came up, the professional journalist next to me had tears in his eyes: "God, they were brave, weren't they." And indeed they were.

Whatever else Catherine McAuley instilled in her sisters, courage is among their greatest attributes, because if it were not for Mother Vincent Whitty, Sisters Catherine Morgan, Benedict McDermott, Cecilia McAuliffe, Emily Conlan, and Jane Townsend who arrived in Brisbane, Australia, in 1861, I may never have learned as clearly as I did that Christian faith is primarily about living compassionately, mercifully.

Before she died, Catherine McAuley's last words were, "Make sure the Sisters have a comfortable cup of tea." By invoking that ritual, which the Irish have made their own, she revealed a faith that is practical, comforting, domestic, hospitable, sustaining, and hardworking. And just like the best of religious faith, it can be dressed up or dressed down depending on the occasion.

ST. MARY MACKILLOP (1842–1909)

Strictly speaking, Mary MacKillop is known as St. Mary of the Cross. She is Australia's first, and at present, only canonized Catholic saint. It is striking that most Australians do not use her formal title, but refer to her by her baptismal name. Maybe it has something to do with Australia's more relaxed and informal style for, even after she was canonized, many Australians drop the

Saint altogether when we speak of her—because good friends rarely stand on ceremony.

It's not that Mary did not know about being crucified; she certainly did. She gives comfort to every sane, rebellious prophet in the church and the world.

While she may have set out to become a saint, something all baptized people are told by St. Paul to desire, she was a most reluctant prophet. A teacher by profession, she was appalled by the poverty in rural Australia and knew that education was one of the great keys to true freedom, especially for the deprived people of the Australian outback. In 1866, with her priest friend and adviser, Fr. Julian Tenison Woods, she founded the Sisters of St. Joseph of the Sacred Heart, for the education of poor children. Within five years, 130 sisters were running more than 40 schools and welfare institutions across South Australia and Queensland. Within a hundred years (along with the Sisters of Mercy), the "Joeys" (as they are affectionately called) were in every tin-pot place in the country.

In 1866, Australia was not yet a federation; that occurred in 1901. However, decades before that event, Mary MacKillop wanted her sisters to be free from the interference of local bishops and to respond to national needs. So she opted for a central, national government for her congregation. Most of the Australian bishops did not like it, especially Bishop Shiel of Adelaide who, believing false allegations that Mary was financially incompetent and an alcoholic, also formally excommunicated her on September 22, 1871.

Shiel was certainly not alone. Of the fourteen bishops in Australia and New Zealand in 1871, eleven wrote to Rome against Mary and her sisters. Only three bishops supported her, and they all belonged to a religious order themselves. Today, none of these men are known, except to historians, but the woman they condemned is given to us as a model of universal holiness. In a dominantly patriarchal church, St. Mary MacKillop was loyal in her dissent, strong in hope, magnificent in faith, and unfailing in her forgiveness of her enemies.

With the excommunication lifted on February 23, 1872, Mary had to set about protecting her work and her sisters. This was aided and abetted through an unlikely conspiracy between a Jew, a Presbyterian, and two Jesuits. (That's starting to sound like the beginning of a joke!)

One of Mary's great patrons and friends was Mrs. Joanna Barr-Smith, a devout Presbyterian, who helped finance Mary's first mother house in Adelaide and paid for her tombstone. To have a Protestant benefactor may have been bad enough at the time, but to call her "my very dear friend," as Mary often did, was dangerous in sectarian nineteenth-century Australia.

One of Mary's other good friends was Emmanuel Solomon, a Jewish man who was transported to Australia as a convict for theft in 1818, and later became a successful businessman, parliamentarian, and philanthropist. He admired Mary's work. When she was excommunicated it was Mrs. Barr-Smith and Mr. Solomon who paid for her first-class ticket on the boat from Adelaide to Rome to petition Pope Pius IX to approve and protect her community of sisters.

Mary's younger brother, Donald, was educated by the Jesuits and later joined the Order, and her own spiritual director in Adelaide was an Austrian Jesuit, Josef Tappeiner. When the twenty-nine-year-old Mary was excommunicated, Fr. Tappeiner was so appalled at what he thought was an invalid and immoral act that he and another Austrian Jesuit, Fr. Joannes Hinteroecker, gave Mary the sacraments in spite of the bishop saying that anyone who communicated with her would suffer the same penalty.

Mary arrived in Rome in 1873. Fr. Tappiener had paved the way for her with introductions to his old Jesuit friend, Fr. Anton Anderledy, who was an assistant to, and later became, the Superior General of the Jesuits. It was Fr. Anderledy who assisted Mary through the Vatican's processes for approving her constitutions, to gain papal protection for her sisters from local bishops, and finally, to be personally received by Pope Pius IX.

I do not know any other person in the church's history who

has gone from excommunication to canonization. Certainly, no one else has done it in 139 years.

One of the least-known chapters in her life, however, is also the one that has the greatest contemporary resonance. In 1870, Mary's religious sisters accused their local assistant parish priest of sexual offenses "committed frequently and with many" against children and women in the confessional. There was an investigation and the priest was found guilty of the offenses. He was sent back to Europe. The parish priest was also condemned for "turning a blind eye" to the abuse.[5] He was removed from the parish and sent to the Bishop's House in Adelaide. St. Mary MacKillop supported the denunciation of these priests, but it incurred the wrath of the sacked parish priest who, the following year, would then be one of Bishop Shiel's closest advisers in regard to her excommunication.

In St. Mary MacKillop, we have an outstanding Christian, who refused to be mastered by her religious masters; a person open to ecumenism and interreligious dialogue, who knew that the best way to tear down sectarianism and religious bigotry is simply by becoming friends; a teacher, who believed that education is one of the best paths to human and spiritual liberation; a passionate advocate, who had to learn *how* to use her networks to win both the battle and the war; and an adult who paid a terrible price because she would not be silent in the face of sexual abuse by clergy.

DOROTHY DAY (1897–1980)

For most of her life Dorothy Day was a heavy smoker. She was many other things besides, but the first thing she did most mornings of her adult life was light a cigarette. She used to give up cigarettes for Lent, but she became so irritable over those five weeks that the rest of the Catholic Worker community used to pray that she would go back on them. Her confessor suggested that she stop giving up cigarettes and ask God for the desire to stop smoking and be good natured. She did. One morning she woke up and did not reach for the pack, and never touched them again. It was all about appetites. She had plenty of them.

Dorothy was born in Brooklyn, New York, on November 8, 1897, into a comfortable family. Although her parents were not religious or churchgoers, Dorothy read the Bible as a child and prayed. She joined the local Episcopal Church choir and was later baptized and confirmed. At college, Dorothy became a journalist and political activist, joining the Socialist Party. She rejected all organized religion. For many years, while fighting causes in the labor movement and for socialist and communist ideas, she had a string of sexual encounters. One resulted in a pregnancy and an abortion. In 1922, she married Barkeley Tober. The marriage lasted a year. In 1925, she moved in with an atheist, Forster Batterham, with whom she had a daughter, Tamar Teresa, born on March 3, 1927. She wanted to have Tamar baptized. Batterham strenuously objected. On December 28, 1927, Tamar was baptized, and Dorothy was conditionally baptized into the Catholic Church. It split her common-law marriage. However, Dorothy remained a friend of Forster for the rest of his life, caring for him in his final illness.

By 1932, Dorothy was writing for the Catholic journal *Commonweal* about unemployment, old age, and sick pensions, and the rights and needs of mothers and children. In 1934, she met Peter Maurin, the man she says founded the Catholic Worker, and she worked on its newspaper. She moved into a Catholic Worker House and continued writing, speaking, advocating, and being arrested for her defense of the poor, Catholic social teaching, and pacifism. She died of a heart attack on November 29, 1980.

Dorothy Day's cause to be declared a saint formally began in 2000. For some people, it has been too slow. Many think that her many sexual partners, failed marriage, and the break with the father of her child before her conversion make for a tough case. It could also be argued that while Dorothy showed due respect to Catholic bishops, they were not beyond her scarifying wit and commentary when they did or said anything she could not reconcile with the highest ideals of Catholic social teaching.

It is true that Dorothy Day did not often speak publicly about her abortion or on this particular right-to-life issue. She was, however, the lead signatory to the Catholic Peace Fellowship Statement on Abortion on June 28, 1974:

> We reject categorically the Supreme Court's argument that abortion is an exclusively private matter to be decided by the prospective mother and her physician.... Indeed, we insist that these positions are all of one piece, stemming from what Albert Schweitzer called, "reverence for life," and the consequent obligation to oppose any policy or practice which would give one human being the right to determine whether or not another shall be permitted to live. For many years we have urged upon our spiritual leaders the inter-relatedness of the life issues, war, capital punishment, abortion, euthanasia and economic exploitation...and to work for their elimination and the establishment of a social order in which all may find it easier to be "fully human."[6]

She also once described abortion as a form of genocide.[7]

In 1977, a fellow Catholic worker, Daniel Marshall, asked Dorothy about her abortion. "I don't like to push young people into their sins....You know, I had an abortion. The doctor was fat, dirty and furtive. He left hastily after it was accomplished, leaving me bleeding. The daughter of the landlords assisted me and never said a word of it."[8] In Robert Ellsberg's *All the Way to Heaven*, he cites a letter Dorothy wrote to a young woman in which she spoke not only of her abortion, but also the psychological legacy it left. "Twice I tried to take my own life, and the dear Lord pulled me through that darkness—I was rescued from that darkness. My sickness was physical too, since I had had an abortion with bad after-effects, and in a way my sickness of mind was a penance I had to endure."[9]

It seems tragic that such a manifestly good woman who lived with the poor and advocated for them for her entire adult life has to be defended in regard to her sexual history. We have not been so reticent about other saints with complex personal histories before their conversions. St. Callixtus was an embezzler and political agitator; St. Thomas Becket was a voracious despot; St. Mary of Egypt was a famous seductress; St. Olga was an assassin; St. Vladimir "owned" a harem; St. Philip Howard was a notorious playboy; and, before she saw the light, the Blessed Angela of Foligno's multiple adulteries were scandalous. For St. Augustine of Hippo once said, "There is no saint without a past, no sinner without a future." He knew about both, for, from his own confessions, he tells us that from the age of sixteen "the frenzy gripped me and I surrendered myself entirely to lust," and later he found himself "floundering in the broiling sea of...fornication."[10] We know he fathered at least one child, a son he named Adeodatus.

Saints give testimony to God at work in their lives, not to personal perfection, and so in Dorothy Day we have a saint who knew about the vacuousness of treating sex as a commodity, the failure of relationships, the tragedy for mother and child in abortion, and the feeling that suicide was the only way to stop the pain. Rather than rule Dorothy out of sainthood, I admire her even more.

Not that Dorothy wanted to be a saint. "Don't call me a saint. I don't want to be dismissed so easily." I just hope that those who focus so strongly on this chapter of her life equally offer such an exemplary example as hers in their witness to a Christian faith that acts justly. For in that witness, she is one of the great role models. In 1949, she wrote what has become a personal creed of sorts:

> I firmly believe that our salvation depends on the poor.
> We believe in, "from each according to his ability, to
> each according to his need." We believe in the commu-
> nal aspect of property as stressed by the early Chris-
> tians....We believe in the constructive activity of the
> people....We believe in loving our brothers regardless
> of race, color or creed and we believe in showing this
> love by working for better conditions immediately and
> the ultimate owning by the workers of their means of

production. We believe in an economy based on human needs rather than on the profit motive....If we are truly living with the poor, working side by side with the poor, helping the poor, we will inevitably be forced to be on their side, physically speaking. But when it comes to activity, we will be pacifists, I hope and pray, non-violent resisters of aggression, from whomever it comes, resisters to repression, coercion, from whatever side it comes, and our activity will be the works of mercy. Our arms will be the love of God and our brother.[11]

I think we should abandon the formal process of canonization for someone like Dorothy Day and return to the more ancient Christian practice of creating saints by public acclamation that gave us such great redeemed sinners and saints like Callixtus, Becket, Mary of Egypt, Olga, Vladimir, Philip Howard, Angela Foligno, and Augustine. Dorothy's canonization will need to be a very simple ceremony, with the poor at the center of it, not outside St. Peter's Basilica, but right in the heart of New York City's Times Square.

HELEN LEANE (1903–1996)

I never knew Helen by her baptismal name. Until I was an adult, I did not even know she had a baptismal name. She was Sister Mary Consuelo to me, a Sister of Mercy in the order founded by the Venerable Catherine McAuley. She was my first-grade teacher. I said in the preface to this book that one of the distinct groups of interlocutors I have on planes were those educated by nuns, brothers, or priests who did not experience a happy time of it. These people are now often lapsed, collapsed, or ex-Catholics, and on long-range flights, I have to hear about their tale of woe in regard to Sister Mary Agapanthus. While some of these horror stories are true, I don't share them because, while I was a little overawed by the nuns, the ones I knew were mostly loving and kind.

In fact, the best thing to come out of the Vatican's investigation of religious women in the United States of America has been the general outpouring of affection by the former pupils and present admirers of nuns. I am not on my own in believing that some of the finest Christians I have ever been honored to meet are women in Catholic religious life.

Helen Leane will never be canonized a saint, though she should be and could be. Let me tell you why. Sister Mary Consuelo was five foot tall and four feet wide. Behind her back we called her Sister Mary-consume-a-whalelo. She was firm and fair. She needed to be. She once told me that in the forty-four years of her teaching career, she never had less than forty children in her class. In 1959, she had sixty-one children in the same room. There were forty-two children in my first grade class in 1969. Can you imagine that ratio now? In the first grade, Sister prepared us for our First Confession, as it was then called, and our First Holy Communion. I remember being so terrified going into the dark box to make my first confession, that when the slide pulled back, I could barely see through the grill. In my anxiety, I started yelling on top note, "Bless me Father for I have sinned, this is my First Confession and these are my sins." At that point, the dean of the Cathedral said, "God's not deaf and neither am I!"

I wish I could say that I was really looking forward to my First Holy Communion because I wanted to receive the Lord in a special and unique way. But that would be a lie. Actually, I was terrified of doing something wrong at the Mass and of biting the host. At the age of seven, what I was really looking forward to was the party that followed the Mass and the presents I would get. Back at school the day after my communion, Sister Mary Consuelo asked me what gift I enjoyed the most. Of all the Bibles, holy pictures, rosaries, and medals I received, the gift I treasured was a bone china holy water font of the Madonna and Child. "I would like to see that," Sister Mary Consuelo said. "Would you bring it to school tomorrow?"

The next day, during the first break, *little lunch* we used to call it, Sister was on playground duty. She was wearing a large blue-

and-white striped apron over her habit. Imagine this scene. There were over seven hundred children in my Catholic primary school, and there was only one teacher supervising all of us—a ratio of 1:700. That would be illegal today. Not that Sister Mary-consume-a-whalelo had any trouble controlling the masses. She was a formidable figure who was as wide as she was tall, and ruled the playground with a whistle. Do you remember how big the nun's pockets were in those habits? Seemingly, the nuns carried everything in them, and they could put their hands on what they needed at a moment's notice. I raced up to Sister, who was surrounded by children: "I've brought the holy water font, Sister." "Very good, go and get it." All wrapped up in tissue paper, I carefully took the font out of my bag and then ran down to the bitumen playground. I was so excited at showing off my favorite present that right in front of Sister I tripped and down I went. The font hit the bitumen too. It did not break. No, it smashed, and into tiny pieces. Sister swung into action. She was an old hand at health and safety, long before the term was invented. Into her pocket she went. Out came the whistle and with a full, shrill blast seven hundred children froze on their spot. Sister said to the children in our vicinity, "Whoever picks up the most pieces of china would get a holy picture." We thought that was something back then.

The second whistle rang out, and while six hundred and fifty children resumed their games, fifty children did a forensic search of the area picking up every piece the naked eye could see and dropped them in the hammock that Sister had made from her apron with her left arm. Meanwhile, I was so distraught that Consuelo's right arm brought me in for a very big hug. Sister had many gifts, but among them was a very ample bosom. In fact, whenever we read about God's deep and consoling breasts in Isaiah 66:11, I go back to grade one. I am fairly certain I made my decision to become a celibate priest at that moment, between Sister's breasts. I was not sure I was ever going to get out of there alive!

The bell went and Sister rolled up the apron and walked me back to class. Three weeks later, she told me to stay in at little lunch. I thought I was in trouble. When every other child had left the room, she opened the drawer of her desk and there, wrapped up in new tissue paper, was a fully restored holy water font. By then, I think I had forgotten about it.

In those days we knew nothing much about the Sisters. They went to Mass, said their prayers, and taught school. Before Sister Mary Consuelo became a nun, however, Helen Leane had done a degree in fine art, majoring in water colors and ceramics. She had taken those hundreds of fragments and spent hours and hours piecing back together my holy water font. When it was set, she repainted the entire object. The only sign that it had ever been broken was the rough plaster of Paris on the back. She could have thrown those pieces away and I would have gotten over it. In fact, I had. However, such was the effect of her prayer life on her relationships, even with a seven-year-old boy; she spent what must have been most of her leisure time for weeks reconstructing a treasured gift. But she was the real gift that day, and it was the best lesson I had from her.

I am not an overly sentimental person when it comes to things, and have been privileged to have studied or worked in Australia, the United Kingdom, Italy, and the United States, but everywhere I go to live, that font goes too. Soon after being ordained a priest in December 1993, I was honored to be asked to preside at the Eucharist at Emmaus, the Sisters of Mercy nursing home in Brisbane. Sitting in her usual spot in the front row was Sister Mary Consuelo, now aged ninety. As part of my homily, I told the other hundred sisters the story of the holy water font. When I was done and sat down, Sister got up from her place and turned around to the others and said, "I told you I was good!" She was very good indeed.

I visited her when I could over the next few years. My last visit with her was in early March 1996. At that time she knew she was dying. She talked about it openly and calmly. I asked her if she was frightened to die. "Oh no," she quickly retorted, "I'm frightened of pain, but I am not fearful of death, because through it I will go home and meet Christ face to face, and hopefully, he will say to me, 'Well done, good and faithful servant—with what you had you did your best.'" As I drove away from her that final day, there was Helen in my rear vision mirror, now a frail wizened figure waving goodbye. I had tears streaming down my face in gratitude for a teacher who never stopped teaching, an adult who simply and appropriately loved kids who were not her own, and a believer who showed me that faith is about living this life so fully that we can even come to see death as an opportunity to hear Christ say, "With what you had you did your best."

BLESSED TERESA OF CALCUTTA (1910–1997)

Christopher Hitchens did a hatchet job on Mother Teresa. The long character assassination that is *The Missionary Position* could be fairly summarized as portraying Mother Teresa as a fanatic, a fundamentalist, and a fraud, a friend of poverty because she was against abortion, contraception, and divorce, and also that she was theologically dogmatic, had blind faith, and enjoyed "the cult of a mediocre human personality."[12] In this context, I do not think it is mean to note that some of the things Christopher Hitchens observes in Mother Teresa can be found, albeit in different ways, in him and his own aggressive atheism: fanaticism, fundamentalism, dogmatism, blind faith in his own version of reality, and enjoying the cult of personality from his own disciples. This seeming psychological projection, rejection of religious belief, legitimate disagreement over the ways to alleviate poverty, and fundamental clash of political ideology is exacerbated by the fact that Hitchens could not abide that Mother Teresa's fame enabled her to raise money to fund her causes and works.

Having largely worked in poor obscurity for twenty years, there is scant evidence that she was working for the poor for the sake of her own ego and for financial reward. It is true, however, that once fame came her way, she used it to speak about social and political issues of concern to her and the Catholic Church, and to raise funds for her work and the quickly expanding Missionaries of Charity. I don't know another activist who would not do the same in regard to his or her causes and organizations. Her style could be abrasive, her administration was haphazard, her accounting was far from systematic, and her educational and clinical care was, and is, basic, but no one has been able to prove that she or her sisters siphoned any money to a Swiss bank account whereby she or others lived in luxury, or that, because her care was rudimentary, it was not better than the alternative for the poorest of the poor. Others may not like her unremitting stance on what is now called reproductive rights, but she was a Catholic of her time and in lockstep with a stark presentation of the Church's teaching.

On reading Hitchens's book, I was left asking what systematic improvements had Hitchens ever achieved in his lifetime on behalf of, for, or with the poor, anywhere. I am unaware of a single achievement. Hitchens's criticism is so extreme he does not make a single positive comment about her. Conversely, I have seen the good work Mother Teresa's sisters have done, and still do, for the poor in several parts of the world. Today, there are 4,500 sisters in 131 countries. Admittedly, my major personal criticism of her concerns how she tended to romanticize the degradation of grinding poverty. In October 1981, on a visit to Washington, DC, she said, "I think it is very beautiful for the poor to accept their lot, to share it with the passion of Christ. I think the world is being much helped by the suffering of the poor people." I can see how this fits into her traditional Catholic theology of reparation and sin, which has developed considerably in recent decades, for while people who are poor have inalienable rights and dignity, poverty is an evil to be eradicated. At the risk of criticizing Blessed Teresa for what she did not do, I am reminded of Helder Camara's famous comment: "When I give food to the poor, they call me a saint. When I ask why the poor have no food, they call me a communist." It is a rare human being who is good at both.

However, there are several unusual things about Mother Teresa's life that are inspiring. The first is that she was a woman who knew what it was to be pushed from pillar to post. Anjezë Gonxhe Bojaxhiu was born into the Ottoman Empire, but in her lifetime she became, by turn, Serbian, Bulgarian, Yugoslav, and Indian, and if she were able to return to her birthplace now, she would discover that she was now a Macedonian. "By blood, I am Albanian. By citizenship, an Indian. By faith, I am a Catholic nun. As to my calling, I belong to the world. As to my heart, I belong entirely to the Heart of Jesus."

Inspired to become a missionary sister, it is not clear how or why she chose the Institute of the Blessed Virgin Mary (IBVM), commonly called the Loreto Sisters. They did not work in her country of birth, but she did know that they worked in India. First, however, she went to the IBVM in Ireland to learn English for her work in India. In 1929, she was sent to the novitiate of the Sisters of Loreto at Darjeeling.

Maybe the constant change of her citizenship, and the extraordinary amount of travel she did for a woman of her time, explains, in some measure, her later attachment to rigid structures while being on the move.

In 1931, she took her vows and was appointed to St. Mary's College at Calcutta for the next fifteen years. Although she was happy teaching relatively well-off girls, it was the poor, literally beyond her gate, who called her. By 1946, she was sure she was meant to serve them in some way.

By 1948, she was given permission to live outside the convent. She dressed in a blue-bordered sari and founded a school for the often homeless children in the poorest parts of Calcutta, teaching them basic literacy. She was soon joined by other women who wanted to work with her; most were her former students. On October 7, 1950, the Missionaries of Charity were officially established. On April 12, 1952, twelve sisters took first vows as Missionaries of Charity, and Mother Teresa took final vows. That same year Mother Teresa opened *Kalighat,* her first home for the dying in Calcutta. She came to national prominence in India in 1948 when Prime Minister Nehru praised her work with the poor. She came to international attention primarily after Malcolm Muggeridge's BBC documentary about her work in 1968, and his 1972 book *Something Beautiful for God.*

In 2007, *Mother Teresa: Come Be My Light* was published. It consists of the letters and other correspondences between Mother

Teresa, her confessors, and superiors over sixty-six years. The editor, Rev. Brian Kolodiejchuk, says that it is "proof of the faith-filled perseverance that he sees as her most spiritually heroic act." I have mixed feelings about this publication mainly because Mother Teresa explicitly asked her spiritual director to "please destroy any letters or anything I have written." She never wanted anyone to read these letters. However, they do reveal an extraordinary insight into her life that makes her even more inspiring.

In 1957, she wrote, "There is such terrible darkness within me, as if everything was dead. It has been like this more or less from the time I started the work....In my heart there is no faith—no love—no trust—there is so much pain—the pain of longing, the pain of not being wanted. I want God with all the powers of my soul—and yet there between us—there is terrible separation. I don't pray any longer." Two years later she said, "In my soul I feel just that terrible pain of loss, of God not wanting me—of God not being God—of God not existing."[13]

There is no evidence in her letters that this sense of God's absence ever lifted. In fact, she kept questioning and doubting her faith, and that she was doing the right thing, for the rest of her life. Her ministry held no consolation for her. Except for her spiritual advisers, no one knew this. Everyone assumed the opposite to be true. In this context, what is extraordinary is that she just kept going, doing her work for the poor in the hope that it was pleasing to God.

My friend and colleague James Martin, SJ, has insightfully observed,

> Few of us, even the most devout believers, are willing to leave everything behind to serve the poor. Consequently, Mother Teresa's work can seem far removed from our daily lives. Yet, in its relentless and even obsessive questioning, her life intersects with that of the modern atheist and agnostic. "If I ever become a saint," she wrote, "I will surely be one of 'darkness.'"... Mother Teresa's ministry with the poor won her the

Nobel Prize and the admiration of a believing world. Her ministry to a doubting modern world may have just begun.[14]

Mother Teresa died the same week as Diana, Princess of Wales, two of the most identifiable women of their day. After her car accident, understandably, the world never saw a photograph of Diana again. One of the most glamorous women in the world was hidden from public sight. Mother Teresa had many gifts, but no one would ever have described her as glamorous. In death, and after she was embalmed, Mother Teresa was permanently on display, even during her funeral eight days after she died.

While she was alive, there was one revelation after another about Diana, but mercifully, nothing much more has emerged since her tragic death. A lot of ink was spilt on Mother Teresa while she was alive too, but only in death have we discovered how long and lonely her life of faith actually was. Because of that she ends up an even more illuminating person.

OSCAR ROMERO (1917–1980)

My first vivid introduction to Archbishop Oscar Romero was at a film premiere. In 1990, Jesuit Refugee Service (JRS) got the rights to have the first public screening of Paulist Production's film *Romero* as a fundraiser. It was a huge hit in every way.

After the success of *Romero*, the following year, JRS decided to have another film fundraiser, this time with *Black Robe*. On the night, and by chance, I was seated directly in front of the local archbishop and his two assistant bishops. Everything was going well in the story of Jesuit Father LaForgue's mission to the Algonquin Indians in 1634 until Daniel, LaForgue's lay assistant, has sex with Annukam, the daughter of the Algonquin chief. I thought that scene would never end! There were two more to come. I wanted to cover the eyes of the hierarchy that I felt were popping out of their heads into the back of mine. I felt like their Excellency's parents. I can't say how *Black Robe* ends. I assume they died a gruesome death. All I know is that the curtain came down on unseen films for Jesuit fundraisers.

When he was appointed Archbishop of San Salvador in early 1977, Oscar Romero was a surprise choice. He was a bookish and quiet man. El Salvador was in upheaval with growing public defiance of the repressive military government. The junta considered Romero a safe appointment. Then three separate events changed his life. The first happened within weeks of him becoming archbishop. A Jesuit priest he knew and admired for his faith and work with the poor, Fr. Rutilio Grande, was killed by the military for his defense of the rights of workers and farming peasants. An old man and a young boy were shot too. The people asked Romero whether he would stand with them as Fr. Grande had done. He did. It changed his life.

The second event came the following year, when three of his fellow bishops put out a letter condemning the popular people's movement as Marxist, and therefore, as being hostile to Christianity. Romero rejected his brother bishops' claims and saw the movement as the people demanding what they had every right to have. Romero was now on a collision course with some leaders within the Church and the state.

The third event came on January 22, 1979, when the largest political gathering ever held in El Salvador was organized. As the unarmed crowd began to pour into the cathedral square, the military police opened fire, killing 21 people and wounding 120 men, women, and children. From then on, Romero's defense of the poor and his advocacy for their dignity and rights became stronger and more international. Romero said on public radio,

> I want to make a special appeal to soldiers, national guardsmen and policemen: each of you is one of us. The peasants you kill are your own brothers and sisters. When you hear a man telling you to kill, remember God's words, "thou shalt not kill." No soldier is obliged to obey a law contrary to the law of God. In the name of God, in the name of our tormented people, I

beseech you, I implore you; in the name of God I command you to stop the repression.[15]

In March 1980, while presiding at the Eucharist, Romero was shot to death.

The first people honored by the earliest Christians, the first saints, were the martyrs, those who gave their lives for the faith. Our faith is built upon their witness. The word *martyr* comes from the word *witness*. In fact, All Saints Day, celebrated throughout the church on November 1, has its roots in "Martyrs Day" of the early church, attested to by a hymn written in 359 by St. Ephraim. The name was changed to All Saints Day in the seventh century. There are three categories into which a person can be declared a saint: as a martyr, a mystic, or by their "heroic virtue." Most saints these days fall into this last group. Although Oscar Romero has not been canonized a saint yet, his cause is back on track, and many consider him a modern martyr.

The aspect of Romero's life that is so challenging is his conversion, not to Christianity, but to the radical call of the Gospel to have a faith that does justice, to the needs and rights of the poor. This process has a name. It's called *conscientization*," where, as we become exposed to a new idea or a situation, we become more disposed to a new way of thinking, or to the plight of the people about whom we are learning. Romero's life is a study in the process of conscientization. He was the least likely social justice reformer, but his experiences, his reflections on those experiences in the light of Jesus' teaching and example, and his relationships led him to be radicalized.

Romero wanted a quiet life, away from the concerns of social inequality and human rights, a life that focused on esoteric questions of philosophical meaning. Through the process of his conscientization, he realized that the Gospel calls Christians to work for the reign of Christ here on earth, not just in heaven. He saw that this reign has social and political dimensions, whereby the dignity and needs of the poor and the most vulnerable must be protected, nurtured, and respected. Furthermore, he found that when the poor have no one to fight for their God-given rights, the Church must be their voice, constructively working for a more just society and reconciling enemies. Romero became the embodiment of what the Church has called its preferential love of the poor, where we exclude no one, but, just as Jesus did, we go to the margins of society and make sure everyone has a share in the good things of the earth: food, housing, education, health, and security.

Prophets and martyrs are often linked. They are put to death because they cannot live any other way. Such is the liberty of spirit, thirst for justice, and witness to truth they embody, they threaten the social and religious leaders of their time and place so much that they have to be silenced. This was exactly what happened to Romero. He did not go looking for death; it came to him.

We know from eye witness accounts that the moment during the Mass at which Romero was shot was the preparation of the gifts. It was an extraordinary moment to die. In the Eucharist, Christians don't just remember how Jesus lived, died, and was raised for them, but that his saving actions are present to us right here and now. We believe this foreshadows what all good and faithful people will enjoy in the banquet of heaven. In a sense, Romero's life was a preparation for the final, simple, but profound gifts he would offer his own people in Christ's name: courage, sacrificial love, and his own life.

We know that just like that of Jesus, Oscar Romero's death was not in vain. He thought he might have to pay the ultimate price: "If they kill me, I shall arise in the Salvadoran people." That is exactly what happened. Romero's death focused national and international attention on the military junta, and along with the work of many other campaigners for social justice, the junta was ousted from power by 1982.

A prayer inspired by Romero:

Nothing we do is complete, which is a way of saying
that the Kingdom always lies beyond us.
No statement says all that could be said.
No prayer fully expresses our faith.

No confession brings perfection.
No pastoral visit brings wholeness.
No program accomplishes the Church's mission.
No set of goals and objectives includes everything.
This is what we are about....
We cannot do everything, and there is a sense of libera-
    tion in realizing that.
This enables us to do something, and to do it very well.
It may be incomplete, but it is a beginning, a step along
    the way,
an opportunity for the Lord's grace to enter and do the
    rest.
We may never see the end results, but that is the difference
between the master builder and the worker.
We are workers, not master builders; ministers, not mes-
    siahs.
We are prophets of a future not our own.[16]

POPE FRANCIS (1936–)

I have a special bond with Pope Francis, and not just because he and I are both Jesuits. In fact, I was hoping to be the
first Jesuit pope, and now I might have to settle on being the second one—which doesn't have the same ring about it! My special
bond is that by good luck and blessing I found myself in Rome as
a visiting professor to the Gregorian University when he was
elected and installed.

On Wednesday, March 13, 2013, I finished teaching at 7
p.m. The first clue that something was happening were the bells.
As the white smoke goes up, the bells at St. Peter's start ringing
and through a centuries-old tradition, the tolling cascades from
one belfry to the next. It took two minutes for the churches
around the Trevi Fountain, where the Gregorian University is located, to ring out the news. I guess a tweet would have been
quicker, but less poetic.

At that moment, a Polish nun in full habit ran past me,

shouting, "*Fumare bianca, fumare bianca.*" Sister was excited, and all of a sudden, so was I. The previous days had seen this extraordinary Catholic theater, where 115 men talked to the world via a chimney stack. Now it was time for the "big reveal"! I can see where real-life TV gets this stuff.

There are moments in your life when the effort is worth it. St. Peter's is a good twenty-five minutes' walk away and it was cold and drizzling, but sometimes you just have to be there. Every road was leading to the Vatican. Even what passes as Roman road rules were in suspension, though it was hard to tell. I am not sure I have ever experienced such a group buzz before. On arrival at St. Peter's Square, a hundred thousand others wanted to see history too. Being a single traveler is often an advantage, and I got a great spot in front of the left-hand Bernini fountain. It's also a prime spot for the huge screen. That proved to be essential!

At 8:06 p.m., the lights went on in the balcony loggia and the crowd went wild. It took another nine minutes for Cardinal Jean-Louis Pierre Tauran, who suffers from Parkinson's disease, to come out and tell us that Jorge Mario Bergoglio had been elected Pope Francis I. Jorge who? I was the only one who knew his name and that he was a Jesuit. Because all mobile phone access went down due to the overload and I knew more than anyone else about our brand-new Holy Father, I became our area's papal expert. I knew that he was archbishop of Buenos Aires, he was seventy-six, a Jesuit, and that he was runner-up to Benedict XVI last time. The rest I made up and sounded authoritative. My new and temporary disciples in the square lapped it up. I was translated into several languages. If only more of my books would be!

Francis stood there alone for what seemed like the cruelest time, helping me realize why royal families never appear on balconies on their own. Never! You can only wave so often, and royal families have a lifetime to practice it. That's why they come in twos and chat and wave and chat and wave. The new pope had seventy-three minutes to learn the wave, and no one with whom to chat. He looked stunned.

There was conjecture about which "Francis," and why. I

started giving out my well-known class on "boy saints whose names begin with *F*," and confidently asserted that it was a complex mix of Assisi, Xavier, and Borgia. A Latvian woman nearby interjected, "No Borgia could have become a saint." She failed my class, but later, my own mark went down as well because we discovered it's not as convoluted as my theory—it rarely is—but that it is all about Francis of Assisi's mission to rebuild Christ's church.

Then we got "*buonasera*" and the Latin Americans went nuts. Understandably. This guy is now the most famous Argentine ever, jumping to first place over Che, Evita, Maradona, and Messi. Now with "Francis" that country specializes in one-name handles too.

He went on to speak as the bishop of Rome "who presides over all the Churches in charity. It is a journey of fraternity, of love, of trust between us." It was not lost on me. He is no ruler lording it over anyone. He is a pastor, and a leader who knows that the best way to get others to follow you is to empower them and lead by example. I felt empowered just listening to him. Before he gave us his blessing, he did something I have never seen a pope do: he asked us to come to silence and pray for him, and then he bent over in a reverential bow, first and foremost before God, but also before us in the square, and before the world. And one hundred thousand people were immediately obedient. Still. Silent. Stunning. We realized that he was a genuinely humble man who understood something about holiness. We all bowed in awe before mystery.

On March 19, a million of my closest friends were back in St. Peter's Square. If cascading bells of Rome herald the papal election, the hovering helicopters announce the papal installation—from 6 a.m. It was part security detail and part media circus. Unlike the cheery bells, those spinning blades are a foreboding fanfare.

With forty minutes remaining before the start of the ceremony, His Holiness appeared and did the rounds of the square in the Popemobile. The applause was muted not because of a lack of affection for the new pontiff, but because you can't clap when you have to capture the experience on your iPhone or iPad. We are so busy recording our experiences, I wonder if we have them.

Pope Francis kissed the obligatory baby, but near to me, he asked the car to stop. In the crowd he saw an older, very disabled man, lying on a stretcher. Alighting, he went over to him and caressed, kissed, and blessed him. At that moment, it felt like we were playing the part of the crowd in Mark 2:1–12. I swear, if that man got up, packed up his stretcher and walked, none of us would have been surprised. As with his sainted namesake, I think this pope sees the poor. He really sees them. We didn't know it, but it was the curtain raiser for the "tenderness" he would speak of five times in his homily.

After the Popemobile returned from whence it came, the warm-up act was the Sistine Chapel Choir. As proud as I am that my Argentine Jesuit brother has become the pope, when the music rolled on, I really wished an Englishman had won the vote. Only a Brit could sack this entire choir and hire a compatriot to come and save the imperfect pitch of the Cappella Sistina. It's not too late. An English choirmaster would be the greatest gift an archbishop of Canterbury could send a pope. Meanwhile, the choir did their best, but their big, fruity, and flat singing was not warming up anyone around me. Wisely, people returned to their iPods. Apple should have been sponsoring this show.

The changes to the liturgy were noticeable: it was simpler and shorter. At eighty-five minutes it was a race through the sacred rites. Using St. Joseph's feast day, and his example in the Gospels, as a point of departure, Pope Francis spoke of how his ministry, and through him the entire church, has to protect creation and the environment. I thought, the climate-change skeptics will love that!

You have to be dead to be canonized a saint, so Francis is no saint—yet. And I hope he is not canonized, or at least not for a very long time. Since we adopted a canonization process, only seven popes have made the grade in a thousand years. There is a current and worrying trend for popes to canonize their predecessors. No doubt they are saints, but I think the tradition of waiting a good while to start the process is very wise. However, Francis has already captured the world's attention, for all the right reasons, believers and nonbelievers alike. Why?

Like Jesus, Pope Francis speaks accessibly, and he knows the power of gestures and symbols. He says the Church should be like a field hospital after battle, tending the major wounds, and that some of our ministers focus on fixing holes in the road, rather than looking at where the road might be going. He told religious that a charism is not a bottle of distilled water, and bishops and pastors that they should smell like the sheep. He tells us that the Church must grow through attraction, not through proselytizing. He says that we need to be "receiving antennas" that are tuned into the Word of God in order to become "broadcasting antennas." He is not reluctant to mention that he has met religious who have hearts full of vinegar, not joy. He speaks of the need for his ministers to show a "cascade of tenderness," and several times he warns against church programs that are concocted in a laboratory, protected, and away from the frontier and the outskirts that would give them credibility. His first trip outside of the Vatican was to the refugee camp at Lampedusa. When he got there he asked the world, in regard to the plight of refugees, "Has anyone wept?…The globalization of indifference has taken from us the ability to weep!"

Since his election, we have heard much about how he likes simpler things: how he rode the bus; cooked his own meals; paid his own bills; only flew economy class; thought that three hundred people could live in the papal apartments; rejected the silk and ermine cape; chose a gem-less, secondhand, silver-plated ring; goes off script; speaks from the heart; prefers lower-key vestments; does not think we are in a position to judge someone who is gay; proclaims that God's mercy is always greater than our sinfulness; and thinks joy is an essential manifestation of faith.

In isolation, these things are irrelevant, inconsequential, and even comical. Taken together, however, they confront a princely mentality whose names are wealth and its trappings, prestige, privilege, and power. Francis is already showing us where true

Christian faith is found: in Christ, who comes to comfort the afflicted and afflict the comfortable.

MY FAMILY (1963–)

Recently my sister said to me, "It's time you gave up on us for material and worked on your fellow Jesuits." Those stories will have to wait for other books. My mother is fond of saying, "Without me, Richard would not have a book or a talk." She is right. I quote my family a lot, because they have been the source of some of the most humorous and most serious moments in my life. It was also from them that I learned how to tell a story. My mother also once said, "I hope people who read your books do not think we're perfect." I doubt that, but just in case, let me reassure the world that my family is a very normal, sometimes quite dysfunctional, family that has seen our way through some big challenges. However, given that the unforeseen journey of my recent books started with my reflections on my sister's car accident in *Where the Hell Is God?*, and going against my mother's and sister's advice, it seems like a perfect conclusion to this trilogy to return to the original inspiration, because they do, in fact, inspire me to be more faithful, hopeful, and loving.

My brother Peter says that he is the forgotten one in our family. Many people who have heard Tracey's story know about my mother and me, and then, on hearing about Peter, say, "I didn't know you had a brother." That would be music to his ears. Peter is also the most normal member of the family: Tracey is a nurse and now a quadriplegic; I am a Jesuit and a priest. Peter, however, owns his own very successful business and has been married to Michelle for over thirty years. They have three wonderful children and two marvelous grandsons. Peter is four years older than me and we are very different people. He was always a natural and good sportsman. I was good at books, debating, drama, and music. I was a huge disappointment to him growing up. He gave up on me the day I was playing football, got the ball, saw all those other boys, who were much larger than me, running toward me, so I ran the wrong way, and threw up the ball at the other end of the field, which allowed the opposition to score. It was the happy end of my football career. Peter had to leave the sports ground, and I went back to the choir.

It was only after Peter got married to Michelle that, as adults, we got to know and like each other. By then, he was over getting me into the backyard and toughening me up! Of all the causes for admiration I have for him, however, the greatest is that for the last twenty-seven years he has been so faithful in his devotion to the care of our sister. Even when he had small children waiting at home, it was a rare day he would not quickly call in to check if Tracey and our mother needed anything done. Equally generous has been Michelle, who, to my certain knowledge, has never once complained about Peter making that detour home. Many other wives, and mothers of young children who need to be bathed and fed, would have had an angry moment. Not Michelle. They have been a generous and loving team to all of us, models of quiet unassuming support and love. Peter is a humble man in every best way.

Tracey has been a quadriplegic for over twenty-seven years. Though she has had some understandably rocky days early on, she is one of the most emotionally even people I have ever met. She is almost always good natured, interested in the world around her, and encouraging. I have lost count of the number of people who have only met Tracey through her or my writings, and who ask how she is. They feel a genuine connection to her. People have told me that Tracey's moving book *The Full Catastrophe* had such an impact on them that, since reading it, when they are having difficult days, they think of her and it helps to put their own problems into perspective. I do exactly the same, but not only because contemplating quadriplegia snaps me back into gratitude for what I have, but also because Tracey's good humor in the face of daily trials challenges me. If she can wake up and get on with the day in good cheer, then I sure as hell can too.

My mother was married eight years when, at the age of thirty-two, she became a widow. Dad was thirty-six. He had a massive stroke. I was actually with my mother when she found out about Dad's death. I was two months short of my third birthday. My father owned a stock and station agency in Warwick, Australia. It was the first Tuesday in August 1966 and that was Dad's day to go to the local sale yards and auctioneer sheep and cattle. There were some clients who would have no one but my father as their auctioneer.

He had woken up that day with a headache, but he did not describe it in any different terms other than that. My mother, a nurse, had given him some aspirin and told him if it got worse to see the doctor later in the day. Dad was actually in the ring auctioneering when he collapsed and died. In a small country town, where my father was a notable and much-loved local figure, word spread like wildfire. At the time Dad died, my mother and I were at a department store in the main street of our town. As we returned to the car from the store, an unknown lady approached my mother visibly shaken and through her tears blurted out, "I am so very, very sorry." My mother thought the woman was terribly confused, or nuts, but it was an unsettling experience, so rather than continue on shopping, we went home. As she drove into the driveway of our house, waiting for my mother at the front door was the priest and Dad's best friend.

Though I can see the scenes I have just described in my head, I don't actually remember them. I have made my mother's retelling of that morning's events my own. I do, however, have one precious memory of that day. Maybe it was seared into my very young memory because of the tsunami of grief that engulfed our house that day. Somehow, I knew to hold onto something from my father that day. All I have is one memory.

Dad went to the front door of our home to say goodbye to my mother and me. I was standing there with my two-year-old arms outstretched for a goodbye kiss and a hug. His headache was acute. He said goodbye to my mother, but he could not bend down to me, so he told me to get up on the big leather club chair we had next to the front door. He was in pain, but he kissed me gently, put his large fingers under my small chin and said, "Always keep the chin up, little boy," and walked out. He left our home, our lives, and this world.

I grew up, therefore, in a single parent family. Can we please stop giving all single parents a hard time? Some are certainly negligent and their children suffer. Many others, however, are heroic in the way they raise their children. Though a classic family home with a loving father, mother, and children is always to be preferred, children of single parent families are not always going to be deprived of the essentials and grow up to be deficient adults. My mother raised her children as best she could, and, then, when we became adults, at the age of fifty-six, she became the primary caregiver for her quadriplegic daughter. Now in her eighties, my mother gets up every night at midnight, 3 a.m., and 6 a.m., and turns Tracey from one side to another. She has been doing that almost every night for the last twenty-five years.

1 John 3:18 says, "Let us love, not in word or speech, but in truth and action" and later in 4:7 John says, "Let us love one another, because love is from God." In the practical, daily, loving actions my family have shown each other, I have seen God in action, and have been inspired to be worthy of such an example.

GLORIA/GORDON (1965–)

As mentioned earlier, St. Canice's Catholic Parish takes in the people of the red light district of Sydney: homeless people, women in prostitution, at-risk children, and substance abusers. The Jesuits have cared for the parish since 1989. Because I have a musical background, when I arrived there in 1992, I announced that I would be refounding the parish choir, and that anyone who wanted to join up should see me after Mass. After Mass, a tall, beautifully dressed woman, wearing a deep blue outfit and a big floral hat, approached me and said,

"Father, my name's Gloria and I want to join the choir. I sing bass."

"Well, Gloria," I said, "It always hard to find basses. You'd be very welcome. See you tomorrow night for our first rehearsal."

As Gloria walked off she stopped, turned, and said, "You do realize I'm a trannie, don't ya' Father?"

"Yes Gloria," I said, "even I had figured that out—it's unusual to find a woman who can actually sing bass."

Gloria was, without question, the worst bass I have ever heard. The only note she had was that sonorous note that some basses get when they sing something like "A-men." Not that my choir was only made up of colorful characters from the red light district. St. Canice's also takes in some of Sydney's most salubrious harbor side suburbs. My bass line was made up of a merchant banker, an attorney, a medical specialist, and a transvestite.

Word about Gloria spread like wildfire around the Cross and soon many of her friends were coming to Mass to see and hear her sing. One Sunday, at the end of a hymn, Gloria let one of those big "AHH-MENs" go, and soon I had two pews of transvestites on their feet yelling out, "You show 'em, girl."

Not everyone in the parish was coping! Some parishioners complained that she was a distraction to their prayer and making a mockery of the Mass. Eventually, the issue came before the parish council. Just as they were about to vote on whether Gloria should be asked to leave the choir, my Irish Jesuit parish priest spoke up. "You know," he said, "in the fourteenth chapter of Luke's Gospel, our blessed Lord says, 'When you give a banquet, go out and invite the poor, the crippled, the blind, and the lame.' Now, if you ask that fellow, confused as he obviously is, to leave the choir, we will never see him or his friends again. And the last time I checked, I thought the sacraments were for those who need them most. Who do you think you are in deciding who the Lord invites to the Mass? But be warned: vote Gloria out tonight, and tomorrow morning the four Jesuits in your parish will have to move out of your precious parish as well. We are broken too, but don't show it as publicly as that fella. Now…go ahead and have your vote."

We won the vote, and Gloria remained.

After three months, Gloria told me that her wife was dying of cancer in another city and she needed help to face up to her problems, sort them out, and return home. I got Gloria in to see a Catholic psychologist. She vanished from the parish for months. Then, one day, a man turned up on the doorstep. I didn't know who it was until he spoke. "G'day Father, it's Gordon and I've just come to say goodbye."

A good while later a letter arrived from Gordon. In it he had asked that his letter be read out at Sunday Mass.

A few weeks ago I arrived home and connected again with my wife and sons. Last night at home, with the three of us holding her she died peacefully of the breast cancer which she had for the last 18 months. After the undertakers took her away and I put our boys back to bed, I just lay on the bed looking at the ceiling knowing I wouldn't have been here if it wasn't for the goodness of the community at Kings Cross. I know it wasn't easy for some of you having a drag queen in your church choir, but you believed in me even when I didn't know who I was, what I wanted and where I needed to go. Because you hung in there with me, I was able to find out what mattered, get some help, come home, nurse my wife to her death, and now be a father to my boys in the way they deserve. Who would have thought that approaching Fr. Richard to sing in his choir was eventually going to play itself out into reconciling a husband to a wife who was a model of forgiveness, and a father to two boys who do not deserve to be orphans?

I am not sure if you are aware how often you sing of, preach and speak about "Amazing Grace." Never stop doing that. I am here as a witness to its power in our lives. If I understood you correctly, Amazing Grace says God doesn't care where we start. It matters where we invite God to finish things—by welcoming in Amazing Grace.

Amazing grace! how sweet the sound,
that saved a wretch like me!
I once was lost but now am found,
was blind but now I see.

Gordon's story enables me to remember that Christianity is the religion of the second chance; that it doesn't matter where you start, but where amazing grace can finish it.

SURVIVORS OF SEXUAL AND PHYSICAL ABUSE BY CHURCH PERSONNEL (1992)

I began this book by saying that the single largest stumbling block I hear about in regard to faith in God is the sexual abuse of children by the clergy. Though in other parts of this book, I have placed this issue in a wider context, I have not run away from the despicable criminality of the actions of a very few church personnel and the cover-up of their crimes by some of our leaders. The fact is that many people have come to some church institutions over the years, in a variety of countries, and have been harmed emotionally, spiritually, and sexually. This is particularly reprehensible because the Church is meant to set the standard of morality, care, and safety for the rest of the community.

I have met several survivors who are living lifelong sentences for what was done to them, and their families are too. Although sexual abuse of children is clearly an issue for families as well as institutions, if the Church is ever going to reclaim its moral voice in society, then it is in need of much healing.

In writing about survivors and their families as people who inspire me, I am not pretending for a moment that they are all faith filled. Far from it, but they started out that way. From the stories of survivors I have heard and read, a unifying theme is that they were almost always devout members of the Church when the abuse occurred. On the one hand, this makes sense: their closeness led to access by the abuser; on the other hand, it reveals the risks undertaken by the abuser, which could only be explained by a profound pathology. Understandably, one of the striking things to note, almost universally, is that when survivors take the witness stand in any trial or hearing they rarely swear on the Bible before giving their testimony. They usually "affirm" to tell the truth. I cannot begin to imagine how their sense of believing in a loving and good God was severed by the actions of a so-called man of God, and how their alienation was later compounded by the Church's denial, obfuscation, and refusal to take responsibility.

In high school, I was educated by the Edmund Rice Brothers, and as a boy, I was around parish priests all the time. Personally and among my peers, I never heard anyone ever suggest anything in regard to sexual abuse. I was more worried about physical abuse, which while strong in those days in Catholic and other schools, was never sadistic, and many of our family homes could be physically tough places too. My ignorance is not surprising because, as we now know, secrecy is another elemental manifestation of the abuse.

The first time the issue of the sexual abuse of children by church personnel entered my consciousness was with the 1992 film *The Boys of St. Vincent*, based on true stories from Mount Cashel Orphanage at St. John's, Newfoundland. This is why I placed 1992 as the year for these reflections. I can remember at the end of that searing film reassuring myself that these cases were aberrant, isolated, and few in number. I went into institutional protective mode. I did not want to know about any more people who had been abused while in the care of the Church. That film triggered public attention throughout the world, especially in regard to orphanages and boy's homes. Allegations, victims, and cases started to mount up. The cases were certainly criminally aberrant, but they were not isolated and not few in number.

Rightly, ever since 1992, believers have been unable to hide. *Primal Fear* (1996), *Song for a Raggy Boy* (2003), *The Magdalene Sisters* (2004), *Twist of Faith* (2004), *Bad Education* (2004), *Our Fathers* (2005), *Deliver Us from Evil* (2006), *Hand of God* (2006), *The Sex Crimes of the Vatican* (2006), *Doubt* (2009), *Sunshine and Oranges* (2010), *What the Pope Knew* (2010), *Mea Maxima Culpa: Silence in the House of God* (2012), *Secrets of the Vatican* (2014), and *Spotlight* (2015) are just a few of the more widely distributed films and documentaries that have partly or fully dealt with sexual abuse of minors by religious officials.

While some of these presentations have distorted, falsified, or misrepresented some facts, and others have dramatized and telescoped events for their own purposes, no one who cares about the Church can minimize the gravity of the crisis anymore. The word *crisis* has to be among the most overused and misapplied words in the English language. Certain politicians and journalists would have us believe that we are in a constant state of crisis politically, socially, and economically. We are not. We have problems, some major ones, and we are trying to deal with them as best we can. Sometimes we hit a crisis that is a make-or-break moment. These are rare. That said, I think the sexual abuse of children is a crisis for all the churches. It is a make-or-break moment for many people in regard to belief, unbelief, membership, and belonging and even whether the churches can be trusted at all, about anything. The stakes are presently very high.

There are two things that inspire me about survivors and their families. The first is that they kept telling the truth when no one wanted to hear it. This often started in their families who were sometimes hostile and disbelieving because they, like many of us, could not believe that a particular priest or brother would be capable of such a heinous act. Then the person or the family encountered an institution that wanted to deny the truth and protect the assets. As we now know, the Catholic Church was not on its own in this regard, just an appalling "exhibit A" of what not to do. The armed forces, government departments, especially those who presided over state-run homes for children, every other Christian denomination, Islam, Judaism, and the Scouting Movement, were all equally self-protective. Leaders often thought that if they ignored the case, which was in fact a very vulnerable and courageous person, it might go away; that the cases were isolated; and that the good name of the institution should be protected above all. Well, look at the so-called good name of some of these institutions now. True repentance and reconciliation starts with telling the truth, no matter how painful it is to say it or hear it. Healing begins with being believed. The rage and courage of survivors and their families, the priests who supported them against the odds, the journalists who reported their stories, the police who began investigating, and the politicians who took on institutional power no matter what; these people inspire me to do what we can now to make amends, work at healing people, if we can, and attend to the institutional root causes that saw the crimes, criminals, and cover-ups thrive.

Furthermore, I do not want to be one of those priests who presume that simply telling the truth and being believed is enough. In the traditional culture of indigenous Australians, when an offense has been committed, the community must do "payback." If the crime is significant, the restitution involves the perpetrator, or the family, spilling blood. In Western countries, the equivalent of spilling blood is through a monetary settlement. It can hurt the individual or the family or the institution. It can be necessary as a way of saying that we are serious about healing and our sincere amendment of purpose. I expect we will be a smaller, poorer church in the years to come, but rightly so!

The second way survivors inspire me is that they have survived. I know of six victims of sexual abuse by church personnel who have committed suicide. I did the funerals of two of them. They are among the saddest services I have ever done. The justified anger toward the Church is felt and expressed. However, funerals are for the living, not for the dead, and these families knew that the Church is greater than the criminal abuser, and that a church service would help them say goodbye and grieve more than any other alternative.

When a victim of clergy sexual abuse suicides, the one question we are *not* left with is "Why?" We know why. Their childhood was robbed from them. Their innocence was taken away. They were left feeling guilty and ashamed. The consequence of this trauma is often chronic depression. Many victims are also *very* good at covering it up, presenting well and even overachieving. It's only in retrospect that many of the person's family or friends remember a conversation, a moment, or an event where they glimpse the shadow—but it is difficult to know its depth. Depression thrives in hidden places, in silence. In either case, sometimes the shadow takes over, or the person we know to have a heart of gold, be loving, fun, talented, compassionate, loses the battle with the heart of darkness.

The research we have from people who attempt suicide and live says that they did not want to die; they wanted the pain to stop. Despite the love and support and the drugs and therapy, the pain inflicted by a trusted churchman becomes too much to bear. They do not rationally choose death; they become powerless in the face of the pain, and can longer live with it.

Other survivors inspire me because at some stage they share the trauma of what happened to them and get the help they need and deserve. Some have a very public battle with depression or other mental illnesses for the rest of their lives, but their families and friends hang in there with them. Others take the trauma and demand justice. They speak for the living, who cannot find their voice, and they speak for the dead. We need them.

THE TRAPPIST MONKS OF ALGERIA (1996)

The Trappist monastery of Notre-Dame de l'Atlas of Tibhirine in Algeria first came to my attention in early April 1996 after seven members of their community were abducted by local terrorists in the early hours of March 27. The Groupe Islamique Armé (GIA) claimed responsibility for their kidnapping and tried to exchange their lives for one of their leaders on April 18, 1996. GIA announced that they had murdered the monks on April 20. The heads of the seven Frenchman were discovered by the Algerian army on May 31. The rest of the bodies have never been found.

John Kiser's moving book *The Monks of Tibhirine: Faith, Love, and Terror in Algeria* told the wider story in 2002, but the 2010 film about the community and its end, *Of Gods and Men*, was where, along with the rest of the world, I came to know only in part and to admire in full the nine heroic men of that religious community. Two survived. One was Fr. Jean Pierre:

I was in my room, in the porter's lodge, out a bit from the seclusion area. I heard some noises. I thought that the terrorists came to look for medicines, as they had done before. I did not move until someone came to knock at my door. I was frightened. But I opened. It was a priest from the Orano diocese who came to tell me that my fellow brothers had been kidnapped. It was a shock, as hard as my sense of confusion. But at the beginning no one thought that they could harm some monks, men of prayer respected by everyone.[17]

Fr. Amédée also survived. Through both of these men we know in detail what happened before and during the events on March 27, 1996.

Of Gods and Men is one of the finest religious films ever. While that's a big claim, I am not on my own in making it. In 2010, it won the Jury Prize at the Cannes Film Festival and later won awards from the International Cinephile Society, London Critics Circle Film, the U.S. National Board of Review, and the César Awards of 2011. Slow and deliberate, this film initiates us both into the world of the Catholic Trappist monastery of Mt. Atlas, as well as into the life of postcolonial Algeria with its corrupt government, extreme Islamist terrorists imposing something like Taliban terror on the local towns and villages, and the ambiguous role of the military.

The Order of Cistercians of the Strict Observance is a monastic community that follows the Rule of St. Benedict. Founded in 1664, the order is a reform movement of the Benedictine tradition, living the Rule, as its name would suggest, much more strictly. The Benedictine Rule breaks up the day into periods for liturgy, community life, meals, reading, and work, where the regular rhythm of life enables the monk or nun to come closer to God. The rigor of Benedictine monasteries is not easy, but Benedict's rule is marked by its gentle tone and compassion, "to establish a school for the Lord's service," (prologue 45) where "we progress in this way of life [that, in his love, God shows us] and in faith," and so "run along the way of God's commandments, our hearts overflowing with the inexpressible delight of love" so that "never swerving from his instructions, but faithfully observing his teaching in the monastery until death, we shall through patience share in the passion of Christ that we may deserve also to share in his Kingdom" (prologue 21, 49–50).

St. Benedict understood the link between liturgy and life. He thought that living life at a less breakneck speed was sane, and he was passionate about savoring things—actions, food, creation, people, and especially words.

Of Gods and Men communicates the life and spirit of that community: the prayer, Eucharist, sung liturgy, silence and contemplation, the detachment of the vow of poverty, the taken-for-granted sacrifices of the vow of chastity, the work, the meals and the readings, the meetings, and social outreach.

What was distinctive about this particular Trappist monastery at Tibhirine was their interaction with, and service of, the local community. The monks were generally loved and respected by their neighbors. They sold their honey and vegetables in the local market, worked to help build houses, and gave any support they could to those in need. One of the monks, however, Brother Luc, was a medical doctor who ran a clinic and dispensary from the monastery. He was the only trained doctor in the area. He served the villages, wounded rebels, and soldiers alike.

It is Brother Luc's letters to his community in France that gives us the most vivid picture of the impending threats. Despite the local esteem with which they were held, the monks were Catholic and French. The rebels sometimes attacked their monastery and regularly made threats. They were frightened, and the religious men seriously contemplated leaving the country. Brother Luc wrote, "The violence here has not abated. How can we get out of this mess? Violence will not cure violence. We can only exist as humans by becoming symbols of love, as manifested in Christ, who, though himself just, submitted himself to injustice."[18]

We now know that the monks had to personally and communally discern whether to stay or go. In the film, and according to the eyewitness accounts, they had vigorous community meetings at which they weighed the options. They looked at what impact their decision would have on their families, the local people, and the opportunity to continue their work elsewhere. In *Of Gods and Men,* one of the monks is traumatized by the enormity of the choice to stay or go, and he endures a "dark night of the soul." His conversation with the prior is one of the most moving scenes in an already moving film. In the end, each monk decides to stay, not because anyone wants an untimely or gruesome death, but because their solidarity for the community, their work for justice and their witness to faith in Jesus Christ, the resurrection and the life, means that to cut and run would be a betrayal.

In what were to be his final weeks, the prior, Fr. Christian, wrote,

> *When an A-DIEU is envisaged...*
>
> *If it should happen one day—and it could be today—that I become a victim of the terrorism which now seems to encompass all the foreigners living in Algeria, I would like my community, my church, my family,*
>
> *• to remember that my life was given to God and to this country;*
>
> *• to accept that the One Master of all life was not a stranger to this brutal departure;*
>
> *• to pray for me—for how should I be found worthy of such an offering!*
>
> *• to be able to associate this death with so many other equally violent ones that have been allowed to fall into the indifference of anonymity.*
>
> *My life has no more value than any other. Nor any less value. In any case, it has not the innocence of childhood. I have lived long enough to know that I am an accomplice in the evil which seems, alas, to prevail in the world, and even in that evil which would strike me blindly. I should like, when the time comes, to have enough lucidity to beg forgiveness of God and of my brothers and sisters in the*

human family, and at the same time to forgive with all my heart the one who would strike me down. I could not desire such a death.

My death, obviously, will appear to justify those who hastily judged me naive or idealistic: "Let him tell us now what he thinks of them!" But these must know that at last my most insistent curiosity will be satisfied. For this is what I shall be able to do, if God wills: immerse my gaze in that of the Father to contemplate with him his children of Islam as he sees them....

And you, too, my last-minute friend, who would not have known what you were doing; yes, for you too I say this thank-you and this "adieu"—to commend you to the God in whose face I see yours. And may he grant to us to find each other, happy thieves, in Paradise, if it please God, the Father of us both. Amen! Inshallah.[19]

Through the accounts of Fathers Jean Pierre and Amédée, we know that the night before their confreres were abducted, the eight monks at Tibhirine were joined by a ninth monk, Father Bruno, from the community at Morocco near Fez. He arrived to oversee the election of the Prior. He brought with him gifts of wine and cheese. It occasioned a celebratory meal, which was to be their last supper. We know they listened to one of the only tape recordings they had, Tchaikovsky's *Swan Lake*. The actual music we hear in the film is from the scene in the ballet where Odette, the white swan, realizes she will always be entrapped because Prince Siegfried has been deceived by the evil scheming of the Odile, the black swan. Odette dies and, shortly after, so does Siegfried, so that in death they achieve the consummation that life could only frustrate. As the wordless scene of the monk's last supper continues in the film, the faces of the men tell the story of the life and death choice that they will soon consummate.

On April 27, Father Christian, Brother Luc, Father Christophe, Brother Michel, Father Bruno, Father Célestin, and Brother Paul were abducted at gunpoint. Fr. Jean Pierre was never discovered living in the porter's lodge. As the terrorists searched the monastery, Fr. Amédée hid under his bed and was not found there either. He died in 2008.

The community guest that night was Father Bruno from Morocco. Though he was aware of the imminent danger his confreres were in, he was not part of their communal discernment. As Father Bruno was taken away, Father Amédée, from under his bed, heard Bruno say to his captors, "But I am just a visitor." That would be my luck too—becoming a martyr with no proximate preparation. However, Father Bruno is the patron saint of all of us: visitors on this earth until we make the final journey home.

CONCLUSION

Dear Tom,

Since our conversation on a plane motivated this book, I think that it's only right to conclude by returning to you.

I admire your sainted namesake, Thomas. I took him as my patron saint at confirmation. However, like me, you may have misread his big moment in chapter 20 of John's Gospel. For most of my life, I thought that doubting Thomas doubted Jesus. He didn't. He doubted the church, and not about a small matter of Christian theology, but about the central tenet of faith: that Jesus was raised from the dead. Being in the wrong place at the wrong time, Thomas missed out on his own experience of the Risen Christ and dismissed the witness of his fellow disciples. I like the fact that, in the intervening week between Thomas's initial doubts and Jesus' reappearance, the earliest church did not kick him out. They held on to him, even while he was filled with doubts and questions, so that he might have his own religious experience. So much so that Thomas goes on to make one of the greatest confessions of faith about Jesus in the New Testament.

Faith is not certainty. Doubts and questions are essential elements of contemporary religious faith. We just have to make sure that we are sincerely looking for answers to our queries. In my reflections, I have argued that our dialogue with atheists can be clarifying for us, as long as they are conducted with mutual respect. In secular and pluralistic democracies, we are all free to accept and reject any religious belief, as long as it respects the rule of law and the rights of others. Though religion should never have the only or final say in society, believers have every right to bring their religious faith to bear on debates and discussions in regard to laws and social policies. Where a particular religious faith is held by the vast majority, then it is not surprising that a country's laws continue to enshrine the majority's values, while always protecting the minority's right to dissent, to further debate the issues, and to protect everyone's human rights and the freedom not to believe.

Though many of the current aggressive atheists often want all Christian believers to be the same, we are not. Just as there are many and various sorts of atheisms, there are many and various sorts of Christians too. Catholicism, the largest single Christian denomination, for example, does not take the Bible literally, and we no longer see science as the enemy of faith. We do not have to choose between the two. They are asking different questions. Science works to explain *how* we came to be here. Religious faith asks *why* we are here, what meaning there is to existence.

For believers, the argument that creation has occurred by random chance is not satisfying, for it is also a significant leap of faith, into randomness. For many of us, the sheer balance within creation and the minute structures of nature argue for a purposeful design and a meaning to existence. To hold that the world and our lives are, in fact, meaningless, and that we are destined for personal and cosmic extinction is, for believers, alienating. For people of faith, religious experience lies at the heart of their belief. While some of our detractors argue it is a form of mental illness, an encounter with one's faith in God is one of the most cross-cultural and cross-generational experiences attested to in recorded history and today.

The appeal to religious experience raises the reality that there are different ways of knowing and different types of evidence. Just as in science there are different, contested ways to know scientific truths, so there is a variety of ways to know God, based on experience, mediated through a community of faith, and with the evidence of how people's lives change and are enriched as a result. Rational knowledge comes in different ways, and not only through the scientific method of questioning, hypothesizing, testing the hypothesis, analyzing results, drawing conclusions, and communicating the results. We know and trust many results in regard to other human experiences because we have encountered or experienced them: love, forgiveness, beauty, and conscience, just to name a few. Like religious experience, just because it is not worked through in the same way that scientific knowledge is, does not make it any less rational. Depending on people's religious experiences and intuitive knowledge of God, images of God and structures around a shared belief have developed. For all the great things religions have contributed to the human community, there is no escaping that some of the consequences of religious belief and doctrine have been, and are, criminal in what it has wreaked upon the created order and the human family. It is important to note that humanity has suffered grievously under atheistic regimes too. There is enough blame to go around for all ideologies.

We argued that while religion has played a disgraceful role in justifying war, no systematic analysis of the causes of war concludes that religion is the only and primary motivation for war. Ideology is born of greed for land or resources, or for political power within cultures, tribes, and between nations. Even though some of our critics can quote texts from the Old and New Testament, the Qur'an, and other sacred texts as positive proof that religion is inherently violent, it all depends on how one reads these texts, sees them in their historical context, and interprets them today. The vast majority of religious believers might hold to scriptures that, in part, speak of violence, but they live peacefully and agreeably with their neighbors. Terrorists use all sorts of ideologies to justify their criminal actions, religious or otherwise. Given that there are around 6.5 billion religious believers in the world, it is wrong to say that the evil behavior of a fraction of one percent of them represents all of us and what we believe.

By making a helpful distinction between truth and fact, Catholics, along with most other Christian churches, read the Bible as a library of books, of varying styles and importance that have some facts within it, but are primarily about religious truths. Many mainstream Christians hold that these truths are tested and contested against the ongoing revelation and work of the Holy Spirit, promised to us in John 16:13, through history, science, theology, philosophy, biblical studies, politics, and social experience.

In this context, Christians affirm that Jesus did not simply and only come to die a grisly death to appease an angry God, but that he came to live, so that through his life, death, and resurrection, all of us might know of our dignity and redemption as individuals and as a human family. For whatever else happened in and through the resurrection of Jesus, we know a timid group of ill-educated men and women from a poor outpost of the Roman Empire were emboldened to go out and change the world of their day, in many cases being prepared to die for Christ. Today, Christianity is at its best when it follows Jesus' own example of preferentially loving the world's poor through our actions in regard to advocating for their just needs, as well as in providing for their education, healthcare, welfare, and pastoral care. We are at our worst through the despicable behavior of a very few church personnel who have criminally abused children given into our care, and in the leaders who thought that the protection of the Church was more important than the rights and needs of the victims and survivors.

Whenever Christianity strays from Jesus' law in regard to the love of God, neighbor, and self, we end up in trouble. This law is the litmus test, through which all things must be judged, including our own religious words and actions. It is the guiding principle of our moral code, including how we use our wealth and property to serve the human family. Not that the loving thing to do is not, sometimes, also the hardest and toughest decision; it is just that our morality is not about laws and rules and social control, it is about the ability to learn from two thousand years of experience in trying to live out Christ's love in the world, not repeating our many and heinous mistakes, naming the things that hold us back from realizing our own potential, and serving others so they might realize their own freedom as children of God. Some of our harshest critics would notice the good we have done, and do, only if, as some of them would like, all organized religion ceased to be. While you do not have to be religious to be moral, some of the most heroic human acts of service in every country in the world are done by people motivated by their religious faith. They walk the talk and cannot be easily dismissed as "nutters."

It is this final group, those who practice what Jesus preached, that inspire me to be better and do better. Mary MacKillop, Thomas More, Pope Francis, Oscar Romero, Mother Teresa, the Trappist monks of Algeria, Dorothy Day, Helen Leane, Catherine McAuley, Ignatius Loyola, survivors of sexual and physical abuse by church personnel, Gloria, and my own family are a few of the many Christian people I know who have taught me that Christianity is not about pursuing happiness, but about being the most faithful, hopeful, and loving person I can be—that we can be. Each of them, in vastly different ways, has shown different facets of living a life of faith—in the joy that comes from it, and its cost.

I am so grateful that on that plane you asked me what I did for a living before I could creatively avoid you. Thanks for initiating the journey upon which I embarked that night. I am grateful that you are my fellow pilgrim, and I hope these thoughts enable you to clarify for yourself what we are doing on earth for Christ's sake.

Richard

NOTES

Chapter One

1. *Philomena*, screenplay by Steve Coogan and Jeff Pope (Spyglass Entertainment, 2013). Based on the book by Martin Sixsmith (New York: Penguin, 2013).

2. Eugenio Scalfari and Pope Francis, "The Pope: How the Church Will Change," *La Repubblica*, October 1, 2013.

3. Christopher Hitchens, "Unanswerable Prayers" in *Vanity Fair* (October 2010) also quoted in Windsor Mann, ed., *The Quotable Hitchens: From Alcohol to Zionism—The Very Best of Christopher Hitchens* (Philadelphia, PA: De Capo Press 2011), 42.

4. Pope Benedict XVI, *Meeting of the Holy Father Benedict XVI with the Clergy of the Dioceses of Belluno-Feltre and Treviso,* Tuesday, July 24, 2007.

5. Nick Spencer, *Atheists: The Origin of the Species* (London: Bloomsbury Academic, 2014).

6. Edmund Burke, "Letter to William Smith," in *The Maxims and Reflections of Burke*, ed. F. W. Rafferty (Whitefish, MT: Kessinger Publishing, 2007).

7. Quoted by Rob Cooper in his article "Forcing a Religion on Your Children Is as Bad as Child Abuse, Claims Atheist Professor Richard Dawkins" in the *Daily Mail*, April 22, 2011.

8. Douglas Murray, "Battle of the Books," in *New Statesman*, July 31, 2006.

9. "Portsmouth Institute, Conference Introduction," by James MacGuire in *Modern Science, Ancient Faith: Portsmouth Review* (Lanham, MD: Sheed & Ward, 2013), 8.

10. John C. Polkinghorne, *Science and Theology: An Introduction* (Minneapolis MN: Fortress Press, 1998), 75.

11. The description for slide 2 presented in a lecture by Francis Collins at the University of California, Berkeley in 2008. See also Sam Harris, *The Moral Landscape: How Science Can Determine Human Values* (New York: Free Press, 2001), 161.

12. See "Obituaries: The Rev. Arthur Peacocke" in the *Telegraph*, October 25, 2006.

13. Sir Ernst Chain, in his public lecture "Social Responsibility and the Scientist in Modern Western Society," University of London, February 1970.

14. Richard Dawkins, *River Out of Eden: A Darwinian View of Life* (New York: Basic Books, 1995), 131–32.

15. Colm Toibin, in an interview with Geraldine Doogue, *Compass with Geraldine Doogue*, ABC, October 20, 2013.

16. Pope Benedict XVI, *Creation and Evolution: A Conference with Pope Benedict XVI in Castel Gandolfo* (San Francisco: Ignatius Press, 2008).

17. Steven Katz, "Language, Epistemology and Mysticism," in *Mysticism and Philosophical Analysis* (New York: Oxford University Press, 1978), 22ff.

18. William James, *The Varieties of Religious Experience*, (Cambridge Massachusetts: Harvard University Press, 1985).

19. Daniel Madigan, "When Experience Leads to Different Beliefs," *The Way Supplement* 92, 1998: 72–73.

20. Sir Roger Penrose, *The Emperor's New Mind: Concerning Computers, Minds and the Laws of Physics* (Oxford University Press, 1989).

21. Terence Kelly, *Reason and Religion in an Age of Science* (Adelaide: ATF Press, 2007).

22. Ian Barbour, *When Science Meets Religion* (New York: HarperOne, 2000).

23. Kelly, *Reason and Religion in an Age of Science*, 162.

24. Marcus J. Borg, *The God We Never Knew: Beyond Dogmatic Religion to a More Authentic Contemporary Faith* (San Francisco: Harper, 1997), 57.

25. *Bruce Almighty*, screenplay by Steve Koren and Mark

O'Keefe, rewrite by Steve Oedekerk (Shady Acres Entertainment, 2002).

Chapter Two

1. Meic Pearse, *The Gods of War: Is Religion the Primary Cause of Violent Conflict?* (Downers Grove, IL: InterVarsity Press, 2007).

2. Sam Harris, "10 Myths—and 10 Truths—about Atheism," http://www.samharris.org/site/full_text/10-myths-and-10-truths-about-atheism1.

3. Clifford Geertz, "Religion as a Cultural System," in *The Interpretation of Cultures: Selected Essays* (London: Fontana Press, 1993), 87–125.

4. See http://www.washingtonpost.com/opinions/fareed-zakaria-islam-has-a-problem-right-now-but-heres-why-bill-maher-is-wrong/2014/10/09/b6302a14-4fe6-11e4-aa5e-7153e466a02d_story.html.

5. Mehdi Hasan, "What the Jihadists Who Bought 'Islam For Dummies' on Amazon Tell Us About Radicalisation," *Huffington Post United Kingdom,* http://www.huffingtonpost.co.uk/mehdi-hasan/jihadist-radicalisation-islam-for-dummies_b_5697160.html.

6. "Theology, Terror and Metadata," *Q&A: Adventures in Democracy,* http://www.abc.net.au/tv/qanda/txt/s4045754.htm.

7. Homily of Pope Francis given at a Mass in the chapel of the Domus Sanctae Marthae with a group of clergy sex abuse victims, July 7, 2014, http://w2.vatican.va/content/francesco/en/cotidie/2014/documents/papa-francesco-cotidie_20140707_vittime-abusi.html.

8. Bernard Lonergan, *Method in Theology* (New York: Herder and Herder, 1972).

9. Richard Dawkins, *The God Delusion* (New York: Mariner Books, 2008), 51.

10. Epistle 10.96, cited in F. F. Bruce, *Jesus and Christian Origins Outside the New Testament* (Grand Rapids, MI: William B. Eerdmans Publishing Company, 1974), 25; Gary R. Habermas, *The Historical Jesus* (Joplin, MI: College Press Publishing Company, 1996), 198.

11. Lucian, *The Death of Peregrine,* in *The Works of Lucian of Samosata,* trans. H. W. Fowler and F. G. Fowler, 4 vols. (Oxford: Clarendon, 1949), 4:11–13, cited in Habermas, *The Historical Jesus,* 206.

12. *Politics,* book three, 13, http://classics.mit.edu/Aristotle/politics.3.three.html. See also Lucy Hughes-Hallett, *Heroes* (New York: Alfred A. Knopf, 2004).

13. See http://www.vatican.va/holy_father/john_paul_ii/apost_letters/documents/hf_jp-ii_apl_15081988_mulieris-dignitatem_en.html.

14. Pope Francis, Apostolic Exhortation *Evangelii Gaudium,* November 24, 2013, 103–4.

15. Catholic News Service, "Italian Cardinal Willing to Re-Examine Delicate Church Positions," http://www.americancatholic.org/features/johnpaulii/transition/CardinalsMartini.asp.

16. Emily A. Wcela, "Why Not Women?," *America,* http://americamagazine.org/issue/5152/article/why-not-women.

17. Joshua J. McElwee, "Vatican Spokesman: Female Cardinals "Theoretically Possible," *National Catholic Reporter,* http://ncronline.org/blogs/ncr-today/vatican-spokesperson-women-cardinals-theoretically-possible.

18. Michael McGirr, *Things You Get for Free* (Sydney: Pan Macmillan, 2000).

19. Richard Dawkins, "A Very Atheist Christmas," *Washington Post,* December 21, 2011.

20. Michael Amalfitano, "Hollywood Ups and Downs," *LA Weekly,* December 18, 1998, 28.

21. Andrew Murray, "Battle of the Books," *New Statesman,* July 31, 2006.

22. Charles Taylor, "The Politics of Recognition," in *Philosophical Arguments* (Cambridge, MA: Harvard University Press, 1995), 225–56.

23. Thomas Aquinas (1225–74) in book 2 of the *Summa Theologica,* outlines out how the divinely infused virtues of faith, hope, and charity are practically applied through the naturally

acquired virtues, which Aquinas came to call the cardinal virtues: justice, temperance, fortitude, and prudence.

24. Baroness Susan Greenfield, "The Quest for Identity in The 21st Century," *Sceptre*, May 15, 2008.

25. "Sex Industry," *The White Rose*, http://thewhiterose movement.com/statistics/sex.

26. Gail Dines, *Pornland: How Porn Has Hijacked Our Sexuality* (Boston: Beacon Press, 2011).

27. John Pugente, *Media Literacy: A Resource Guide* (Government of Ontario, 1989).

Chapter Three

1. Dan Madigan, "Muslim-Christian Dialogue in Difficult Times," unpublished paper, Chicago, August 2014.

2. The Trial of Sir Thomas More, Knight, Lord Chancellor of England, for High-Treason in denying the King's Supremacy, May 7, 1535. From *A Complete Collection of State Trials and Proceeding Upon Impeachments for High Treason* (London, 1719).

3. Hugh Mackay, *The Good Life: What Makes a Life Worth Living?* (Sydney: Macmillan Australia, 2013), 12ff.

4. Ignatius of Loyola, "Prayer of Generosity," translated and adapted by Daniel Madigan, SJ. Unpublished sheet music housed at Catholic Institute of Sydney, Veech Library Music by Christopher Willcock, trans. by Daniel Madigan. OCLC Number 224395328.

5. Letter of Father Joseph Tappiener, SJ (South Australian Mission) to the Father General of the Jesuits, October 30, 1872 in *Letters and Documents in 19th Century Australian Catholic History*, ed. Brian Condon (Adelaide: College of Advanced Education Press, 1983).

6. "The Catholic Peace Fellowship Statement on Abortion," *Catholic Peace Fellowship*, http://www.catholicpeacefellowship .org/nextpage.asp?m = 2589.

7. "Do not be conquered by evil but conquer evil with good" January 9, 2010, http://dorothydaytranscripts.wordpress.

com/2010/01/09/do-not-be-conquered-by-evil-but-conquer-evil-with-good/.

8. http://americamagazine.org/content/all-things/dorothy-day-and-abortion-new-conversation-surfaces.

9. Robert Ellsberg (ed.), *All the Way to Heaven: The Selected Letters of Dorothy Day* (Milwaukee: Marquette University Press, 2010).

10. Augustine, *Confessions* (London, UK, Penguin 2003), ii.

11. Day, Dorothy. "Beyond Politics" in The Catholic Worker, November 1949, 1, 2, 4. The Catholic Worker Movement. http://www.catholicworker.org/dorothyday/Reprint2.cfm?TextID=166.

12. "Mommie Dearest: The pope beatifies Mother Teresa, a fanatic, a fundamentalist, and a fraud" www.slate.com/articles/news_and_politics/fighting_words/2003/10/mommie_dearest.html.

13. James Martin, *My Life with the Saints* (Chicago, IL: Loyola Press, 2010), 171.

14. http://www.nytimes.com/2007/08/29/opinion/29martin.html.

15. Quoted from the film *Romero*, (1989). Directed by John Duigan. Also quoted in Danny Saiers, *People of the Sugarcane: The Indigenous People of Northern Cuscatlan El Salvador* (iUniverse, 2008), 215.

16. The words attributed to Monsignor Oscar Romero and often called the "Romero Prayer" were written by Bishop Ken Untener in honor of Romero in 1979.

17. From the film *Of Gods and Men*. It can also be found on the Missionline website: Brother Jean Pierre, the last surviving monk, speaks. "A living inheritance, from Tibhirine to Midelt" by Anna Pozzi http://www.missionline.org/index.php?l=en&art=3349.

18. John Dear, "Easter with the Monks of Tibhirine," *National Catholic Reporter* (April 26, 2011).

19. Quote from Father Christian in Basil Pennington, OCSO, "Cistercian Martyrs of Algeria 1996" in *Review for Religious*, Nov-Dec, 1996. See also: http://www.lovingjustwise.com/martyrdom.htm.